INSIDE DEAF CULTURE

Carol Padden

Tom Humphries

INSIDE
DEAF
CULTURE

Harvard University Press

Cambridge, Massachusetts

London, England

Design by Marianne Perlak

First Harvard University Press paperback edition, 2006

Library of Congress Cataloging-in-Publication Data

Padden, Carol.
    Inside deaf culture / Carol Padden, Tom Humphries.
        p.   cm.
    Includes bibliographical references and index.
    ISBN-13: 978-0-674-01506-7 (cloth)
    ISBN-10: 0-674-01506-1 (cloth)
    ISBN-13: 978-0-674-02252-2 (pbk.)
    ISBN-10: 0-674-02252-1 (pbk.)
    1. Deaf—United States—Social conditions.   2. Deaf—United States—History.
    3. American Sign Language—History.   I. Humphries, Tom (Tom L.)   II. Title.

HV2545.P35   2005
305.9'082'0973—dc22   2004051135

Contents

INSIDE DEAF CULTURE

Introduction
The Lens of Culture

We wrote our first book, *Deaf in America: Voices from a Culture,* to explain the use of "culture" as a way of describing the lives of Deaf people. The term had long been used to describe the practices of hearing communities around the world, but it had never been widely used to describe Deaf people. In 1980, as the idea was beginning to circulate among Deaf people, we took on the task of explaining how a group of people who did not have any distinctive religion, clothing, or diet—or even inhabit a particular geographical space they called their own—could be called "cultural."

We used a definition of culture that focused on beliefs and practices, particularly the central role of sign language in the everyday lives of the community. This characteristic, among others, distinguished Deaf people from hearing people and from other deaf and hard-of-hearing people (such as those who lost their hearing late in life) who do not use sign language but rely on different communicative adaptations. Following James Woodward's example, we adopted the convention of using the capitalized "Deaf" to describe the cultural practices of a group within a group. We used the lowercase "deaf" to refer to the condition of deafness, or the larger group of individuals with hearing loss without reference to this particular culture. Using this distinction, Deaf people range from those who are profoundly deaf to those who hear nearly well enough to carry on a conversation in spoken English and use the telephone, called hard of hearing. We retain this distinction here.[1]

In 1912 George Veditz, a Deaf man about whom we will say more in a later chapter, wrote about himself and his community as "first, last, and for all time, the people of the eye."[2] He did not yet have a vocabulary to describe Deaf people as having a "culture," as we do today. But his sense that Deaf people's lives revolve around the visual and that they engage in practices associated with seeing is one element of what we tried to capture as we wrote about Deaf culture. We drew from his idea of Deaf people as guided by some central core of "seeing," but we stated more: Deaf people's practices of "seeing" are not necessarily natural or logical, in the sense that they have a heightened visual sense, but their ways of "seeing" follow from a long history of interacting with the world in certain ways—in cultural ways. This history involves the schools they attended, the communities they joined after leaving school, the jobs they had, the poetry and theater they created, and finally the vocabulary they gave themselves for describing what they know.

As we look back at how we wrote about Deaf people in that book, we recognize that we were writing not as anthropologists, but as agents of a changing discourse and consciousness, as we tried to model a new vocabulary to describe the community. Through the 1970s, we had each personally experienced a dramatic change in ideas about sign language. For most of our lives until that time, we had called our language "the sign language," as did our family and friends at the time, but with the advent of scientific studies on sign languages, our language acquired a new name, "American Sign Language" or "ASL." The name placed it in the class of human languages, and commanded a different view of its history. The redefinition also made clear that there were many different signed languages around the world, each with a different structure and history, from Japanese Sign Language to Ugandan Sign Language to Brazilian Sign Language. American Sign Language is used in the United States and in English-speaking areas of Canada, and is distinct from other European signed languages including British Sign Language, whose history does not intersect with ASL. With the new definition, we could explain why sign languages and spoken languages have different histories. British Sign Language is not related to American Sign Language because of a fact about schools for deaf children: the first deaf school in the United States was founded in 1817 not by a Deaf British signer, but by a Deaf French signer, whose influence on ASL can still be seen today in some of the vocabulary ASL shares with the French sign language, LSF.

In our first book, we wrote with the express purpose of reframing the practices and ideas of the community as "Deaf culture." At the time, the idea of "culture" gave us a useful construct for describing the varied ways of life of Deaf people in the United States. We used narratives, poetry, popular stories, and other texts to argue for the vitality of a culture embedded within the larger population of deaf and hard-of-hearing people in the United States. Adam Kuper observes about the word "culture" that it is "always defined in opposition to something else."[3] For us, the term culture allowed us to move away from what we and our colleagues believed was a debilitating description of deaf people as having specific behaviors or ideas about themselves or others that were the consequence of their not being able to hear. We cringed at scientific studies that tried to match degrees of hearing loss with specific social behaviors, suggesting an uncomplicated relationship between hearing loss and behavior. We argued instead that being Deaf, the specific and particular way of being, was shaped powerfully by shared histories.

We had begun to write the first part of what we now understand as "the promise of culture." The concept of culture reframed for us the idea of being Deaf, and allowed us to explore Deaf people's long tradition of language and history as a way of understanding their lives. We had some privilege of entry: Both of us are deaf, and we use ASL as our primary language. We have family members who are Deaf, and our lives are lived within the community. Some of the narratives we used to illuminate Deaf people's culture were mined from family members, friends, and colleagues as well as acquaintances in the community. As we probed their meanings, we began to discover threads of connection between the different narratives, across even different generations of Deaf people. We wanted to write a book that would shift away from describing hearing loss as a basis for describing being Deaf. Using Clifford Geertz's memorable description that "one of the most significant facts about us may finally be that we all begin with the natural equipment to live a thousand kinds of life but end in the end having lived only one," we wanted to describe how Deaf people in America ended up living the lives they do.[4]

When we began writing *Deaf in America* in 1984, our community was still reeling from the effects of cultural change. Chief among them was a growing recognition of ASL, which led to a public fascination with language in sign. While it was certainly exhilarating to see the signing of many generations of Deaf people described as a "natural language," we also saw that the change caused a great deal of conflict.

The idea of "Deaf culture," too, caused anxiety. Disbelieving hearing people aside, Deaf people argued among themselves, sometimes bitterly and heatedly, over whether ASL was truly a "language" and whether "Deaf culture" was actually a culture or a "subculture." It would be easy to dismiss these conflicts as examples of denial, or to conclude that when faced with the possibility of a new vocabulary to describe themselves, Deaf people rejected it out of an anxiety over change. Now, however, we can look back on the last thirty years and see an arc of dialogue—and recognize what we have written about in our other work as the historical progress to a consciousness about the Deaf self that provides a way of talking about being Deaf and living with others. "Deaf culture" is no longer the odd phrase it once was. Indeed it has become deeply entrenched in Deaf life; we are sometimes startled to see job advertisements for teaching or social service positions that require the candidate to possess "knowledge of Deaf culture." Young Deaf people today use the term without a hint of the self-consciousness that we had when we first began to use it. What a difference twenty years can make.

From the 1980s until today, we have watched the expansion of the term "Deaf culture" into new and unexpected areas, notably in literature and websites on cochlear implants and genetic research. A recent publication in a genetics journal referred to some "culturally Deaf individuals" who reported in a survey to have strongly negative attitudes toward genetic testing.[5] This is what we write about in this book, the second part of "the promise of culture." In this book, we explore conflicts, tensions, and contradictions in the idea of Deaf culture. This is the other side, where the idea of culture has delivered on *some* of its promise as evidenced by how widely it is used by Deaf and hearing people, but also has brought to the surface strains and tensions. We believe some of these tensions are quite old, as we will show in the following chapters, while others are new. With a maturity that comes from a discourse of culture that we have participated in over the past thirty years, we now feel able, as we might not have been when we wrote the first book, to examine some of the effects and consequences that came from this rapid shift in how we and other Deaf people see ourselves.

The chapters that follow are not a history of the Deaf community in the United States, but a selection of cultural moments in our history. It is not a history because it does not provide a deep description of events from the time of the founding of the first schools for deaf children in the United States to the present. Nor does it cover all the significant events of the community's history, or even most of them. There are very good histories by others that we have relied on heavily to write our chapters, and throughout we refer our readers to these texts. What we have done in this book is to select a sequence of moments that we believe have been profoundly influential in shaping the modern Deaf community, arranged in chronological order from 1820 to the present. We chose these moments because we believe they resonate very much today, and are used by Deaf people as they navigate their path into the future.

Some of this cultural history is well-known to the community— for example, the founding of the first school for deaf children in Hartford, Connecticut, in 1817, which brought isolated groups of deaf children together into a larger community and led to the emergence of American Sign Language. But some of Deaf people's history is less well-known. Only a few months after the third school for deaf children was founded in Philadelphia in 1820, its board of directors received a shocking allegation that their new principal had "inappropriately touched" female students. The incident, which we describe in Chapter 1, foreshadowed nearly two centuries of dominance and control of bodies by institutions established by hearing people for the care and education of Deaf children. It is a history that is silent and shameful, and full of conflict. Yet today, many Deaf people talk with respect about schools for the deaf, even as they acknowledge the sordid history of abuse in deaf schools. Others say they have been wounded by years of repression during their childhoods. For Deaf people to hold at the same time respectful and painful attitudes about deaf schools is the kind of conflict and contradiction we want to explore in this book.

In the chapters that follow, we describe moments that we believe cast a long shadow on Deaf people's history, on the problem of deaf bodies, the problem of voice and self-expression, and the struggle for community. Deaf people's bodies have been labeled, segregated, and controlled for most of their history, and as we will argue, this legacy is still very much present in the specter of future "advances" in cochlear implants and genetic engineering. We explore moments of great anxiety when threats to "eliminate" signed language almost took over deaf education at the turn of the twentieth century. We look at films and other texts to understand how the community valiantly argued for the continued existence of signed language. As a community made up of some individuals who do not speak and some who do, some who do not hear at all and some who hear some, and all of whom draw the label of "disabled" by the larger community, Deaf people are seen as clearly not like anyone else. This feeling of being from a small, different, and exotic group colors the lives of Deaf people. We often feel besieged, controlled, and patronized, even as our remarkable sign language is celebrated and admired in public. George Veditz worried in 1913 about the future of sign language, and still in 2004, we worry. Deaf people were then, and remain today, subjects of all kinds of investigations—sometimes with powerful consequences as in the linguistic investigation of sign languages, but also with worrisome consequences as when medical professionals advise some parents with deaf children that they shouldn't allow their children to sign if they wish them to learn to speak.

We write about the changing work lives of Deaf people in the middle of the twentieth century and what consequences such changes had for the social and cultural lives of Deaf people toward the end of that century. We also write about moments when sea changes occurred that reshaped the ways Deaf people presented themselves to the hearing public, such as when Deaf theater added hearing actors on the stage to give voice to their performances in 1967. As we interviewed family members, friends, and colleagues about the middle of the century, we became acutely aware of the passing of a generation, of Deaf men and women who are in the twilight of their long and eventful lives. Nearly all of them attended schools for the deaf. They eagerly filled jobs left vacant by men and women who left for the Second World War, and when the war was over and soldiers returned, many had to find other jobs. Some became active in Deaf clubs and associations, building a foundation for the Deaf community's advocacy efforts today. Their stories are rich with sentiment and sometimes irony, but always return to similar themes of independence, self-sufficiency, and self-determination. This book is in part a way to remember a generation whose stories can still be told, but not for much longer.

We purposely left out our personal histories in our first book because we were uncomfortable with descriptions of deafness and deaf people that focused intensely and, we believed, too voyeuristically on the deaf experience. It seemed to us that there were, on the one hand, scientific books about deafness and hearing loss, and on the other, personal stories about deaf people born deaf or losing their hearing, overcoming their deafness, and becoming successful despite their handicap. One side was cool and professional, the other emotional and occasionally, maudlin. We were suspicious of a tradition of writing about Deaf people as *objects* of description, but not as *masters* of their own description. As we described the pursuit of understanding culture in general and Deaf culture in particular, we carefully left our personal lives out of the picture, even as we made brief references to our backgrounds—Tom lost his hearing at age six and spent his childhood as the only deaf person in a small rural town in South Carolina, and Carol grew up in a Deaf family in the Washington, D.C., area.

We understand now that our personal lives are intertwined in the very same history we describe in this book and that we too are implicated in "the promise of culture." Jim Clifford, an anthropologist, describes this kind of conflict as "the state of being in culture while looking at culture."[6] We write about the very thing that we live every day of our lives, and "culture" is not merely an abstraction for us. In the last chapter we describe some of our experiences and trace how we have been affected by the changes our community has experienced.

As we mentioned earlier, we could have selected many important moments for this book, but we believe the ones we chose illustrate the common experiences of the American Deaf community since it first came into being over two centuries ago. We are interested in issues of power and dominance in the relationships between groups of people, in part because of our own academic interests, but also because as a very small community living within a much larger country of hearing people, these issues are unavoidable. Deaf and hard-of-hearing people who use ASL as a primary language in the United States and in English-speaking areas of Canada have been variously estimated at between 100,000 to 300,000 individuals. This makes Deaf people in the United States more numerous than primarily French-speaking people in this country (that is, those who use French at home rather than English), but certainly less numerous than other minority language communities such as the Spanish-speaking community. Like other language communities, Deaf people battle for language rights, and like other disabled people, Deaf people dislike being viewed only as medical objects in need of treatment. Battling against dominance and control is a primary theme in modern Deaf life, and it is one we write about in this book.

As we write about the history of Deaf people's ideas of themselves as they confront the powerful ideas of others, we are mindful of this legacy as we look to the future. We write to offer some context for how to think about Deaf people's future especially while science is making plans for our future as well. As classes in ASL reach even higher levels of popularity in the United States, new discoveries are being made about the genetic bases of deafness. Cochlear implants are no longer experimental, but are routinely offered to parents of deaf children. We exist in a time of re-

spect and celebration for difference, yet there is an unending drive
to repair and replace. In 1913, George Veditz worried about a rising
drumbeat of intolerance for sign language and urged us to preserve
the language "for coming generations of Deaf people." Deaf people
carried out his mission and preserved the sign language for a century more. Indeed, we have brought to the language an unprece-
dented level of respect. Somewhere in our present, among the details of our lives and our history, there must be a way to the future.

1

Silenced Bodies

At first glance the Maryland School for the Deaf looks like an elite preparatory school. Large brick buildings surround a campus of smooth green lawns and carefully cultivated flower beds. Massive old elms shade every corner of the campus. At the center of campus stands an old Revolutionary-era military barracks that once housed young deaf children. A water fountain is located nearby, with sidewalks stretching in every direction, linking one building to the other, from the high school building to another for parent education, from the elementary building to the career education training center across the street. On one side of the campus are dormitories where the boys and girls live during the week. The campus occupies two long blocks in the heart of historic Frederick, one of the oldest cities in the state.

Looking closer, there are more hints of the long history of the school. The front of the campus is bordered by a tall, black wrought iron fence punctuated by large brick columns, framing the entrance to campus. There once stood a tall and imposing building behind the fence, but it has since been torn down and replaced with a newer, more modest brick building. Built shortly after the school was founded in 1868, the Old Main Building stood nearly a hundred feet tall, adorned with white-painted turrets and a black slate mansard roof.

Until the late 1960s, most deaf children in the United States were educated in separate schools like the Maryland School for the Deaf. Nearly every state in the country had at least one school for deaf children, and some states had several. The story of these schools is in part about the history of deaf education in the United States, but it is also about deaf children being brought into the care and responsibility of "asylums" and "institutions." The schools were first built in the early nineteenth century as a response to the problem of what to do about deaf children living among hearing people. At first schools deliberated over how to take responsibility for deaf boys and girls, what they should do while they were in school, and how they should interact with their teachers and other caretakers in the school. But quickly it became a problem of "bodies," how to control and manage the lives of deaf children within the school.

Though the Maryland School was built later in the nineteenth century, its architecture and design were typical of many schools for the deaf that were built earlier. The stately Old Main Building at the Maryland School for the Deaf housed the school administration as well as classrooms and sleeping quarters. It was torn down a hundred years after it was built because by the 1960s, buildings of this type had begun to fall out of favor.[1] They were too large, too old, and too reminiscent of an older style of education. In 1950, almost 85 percent of all deaf children attended schools for the deaf, but by 1988, the number had dropped by more than half to 40 percent.[2] By 2002, the number showed more decline, with only 27 percent of all deaf and hard-of-hearing children attending "special schools or centers."[3] The rest attend public schools in "mainstreamed programs," where they are educated with hearing children.

Deaf people in the United States are divided between those who grew up at a time when schools for the deaf were the expected means of receiving an education, and those who were born after the 1960s, when their parents could choose between a residential school or living at home and attending a local public school. It is still customary for older Deaf people to introduce themselves to each other by which school they attended: "I'm from Berkeley," meaning from the original campus of the California School for the Deaf founded in Berkeley in 1868, or "from St. Mary's," a Catholic school for the deaf in Buffalo, New York. The younger generation are more likely to say they went to a "mainstreamed high school" in their home state, which could mean any one of a large number of small programs for deaf and hard-of-hearing students located in a public school. Of the smaller number of Deaf people who attend modern schools for the deaf, they often follow tradition and refer to the school's location as being where they are "from."

The long history of schools for the deaf, lasting nearly 180 years, has left an enduring legacy in the Deaf community. Though now two generations removed, it is a powerful and conflicted legacy, such that Deaf people find it hard to talk about the past and the future of deaf schools without a great deal of emotion.

Some Deaf people will say they believe in special schools and relocate near one so they can send their Deaf children there. At the same time, others intensely dislike special schools and will refuse to send their children there. For some, the intensity of their feelings is personal. Their own experiences as children in such schools has left an indelible impression on their adult lives. They remember the oppressive environments of their classrooms and dormitories, the long separation from parents and family, and living for months with other children without love or affection from adults. One Deaf woman remembers what she calls the petty and irrational rules of her dormitory supervisor, who required that toothbrushes be lined up in the bathroom and shoes be placed directly in front of clothing cabinets. Every aspect of her school life was regimented; punishments were meted out on a regular basis for small and large infractions. She was more fortunate than most in that she had Deaf sisters at the school, but she deeply missed being with her family at home. Today, she says her experience as a child influenced her decision not to send her deaf children to a special school.

Another Deaf woman remembers a brutal "house mother" who locked her charges in a dark closet as punishment. Memories of schools for the deaf in the 1940s and 1950s are almost universally about irrational punishments, moving about in groups, standing in lines, fighting to get a second helping of dessert, waking in the morning to flashing lights and banging on metal beds, sharing showers and sinks. One Deaf man described his residential life with other boys as a "Lord of the Flies" existence, where there were hierarchies of status among the boys, and punishments exerted from within the group of Deaf boys, as well as by their caretakers. He admired his younger Deaf brother who had emerged as a skillful leader at the school; with this brother's "protection," he fared better than some of his friends.

At the same time there are those who believe they were "rescued" by schools for the deaf, and their memories are of leaving behind unbearably lonely homes for an environment of friends and adults who could sign and communicate with them. One eighty-year-old Deaf man we interviewed lost his mother when he was five and was sent to live with his hearing aunt on a family farm during the Depression. He hated the summers of grinding labor, but worse, he could hardly bear the oppressive solitude among his hearing relatives. His Deaf father rarely visited, leaving him entirely in the care of relatives who were exhausted from hard farm labor and had little left to give him. From 1928 to 1940, when he left for Gallaudet, he lived at his school from September to June, and returned to his aunt's farm only during Christmas and in the summers, even though the farm was but a thirty-minute drive from the school. For him, the school became a respite and the closest semblance of family that he could imagine.

Others remember seeing deaf children who were not sent to a school for the deaf, but stayed at home instead. Living and working in the family, they used only home signs, or gestural communication, and lived a life of dependence on their parents. Nathie Marbury remembers in her childhood home in Pittsburgh seeing a girl silently watching from a window of a neighboring house but never joining the children in play. Years later as an adult, she discovered that the girl was deaf and had been kept in her room at home. To this day, Marbury wonders if her own life might not have turned out as well if she hadn't enrolled in the Western Pennsylvania School for the Deaf at the age of six. Born into a large family where there were few resources for each child, Nathie credits the school with giving her the possibility of an education.

Even in the modern context, schools for the deaf continue to "rescue" children, particularly adolescents who struggle to succeed in public schools. Even at a time when distances are short, and information is easy and readily available, isolation still happens. Instead of being caused by geographical remoteness or family income, isolation can be caused by neglect, indifference, or simply lack of expectation. It is not uncommon to find ten- or eleven-year-old deaf children who arrive at schools for the deaf barely literate, knowing not even how to spell or write their last names.[4] Deaf children can still fail to be educated even when surrounded by children or adults.

Deaf people describe schools for the deaf as places where they lived, and indeed, they were designed as such: as buildings where every function of the child was given a designated space. As Deaf children moved from their sleeping quarters to their classrooms to the dining halls, they were imprinted with a strong sense of where they were, and why they were there. The memories of such rigidly organized schools is palpable, but what they also reveal is a sense of belonging with other children who sign, and whose lives are remarkably like their own. When Nathie Marbury contemplates the possibility that she could have been left behind to live in a room alone, as her deaf neighbor was, it is enough to bring tears to her eyes.

It would seem that schools for the deaf today find themselves in a precarious existence as they carry their nineteenth-century lega- cies into the twenty-first century. At the end of the nineteenth century, there were eighty-seven schools for the deaf throughout the country.[5] Since that time, over a third of them have closed, and a few others will probably close soon. Despite a pattern of decline, however, some deaf schools have experienced a revival in enroll- ments. Maryland School for the Deaf, and the California School for the Deaf (since relocated to Fremont), have both had increases in enrollment and are among the largest of such schools. To be sure, they are careful to represent themselves not as "institutes" but as "special schools" or "centers," as they seek to reinvent themselves in a new era of deaf education.

The first school for the deaf in the United States was founded in Hartford, Connecticut, at the urging of Mason Cogswell, an influ- ential philanthropist who wanted an education for his deaf daugh- ter. Disappointed at his daughter's progress with a tutor and in- trigued by reports of successful schools for the deaf in Europe, Cogswell formed a committee of fellow philanthropists and civic- minded colleagues to explore the possibility of a new institution in America for the education of deaf children. He enlisted Thomas Hopkins Gallaudet, a member of his intellectual circle, to travel to Europe to study methods of educating the deaf, and bring back rec- ommendations for instruction at the school. Gallaudet traveled first to England but when he failed in his attempts to visit the Braidwood Schools there, he went instead to Paris where Abbé Sicard invited him to observe the national school for the deaf that he directed on the rue Saint-Jacques. Gallaudet knew that

Abbé Sicard had taken over the directorship of the school from the Abbé de l'Epée, whose reputation in deaf education was known throughout Europe and in America.[6]

At Saint-Jacques, Gallaudet met Laurent Clerc, a deaf former student at the school who had become a teacher, and decided that instead of attempting to learn entirely the methods employed by Sicard and Clerc at their school for the deaf, he would persuade Clerc to return to the United States with him and guide the school's formation. Clerc agreed, a decision that set the course of deaf education in the United States. The failure of Gallaudet to learn from the Braidwoods, who espoused a strictly "oral" philosophy of education, and his subsequent meeting with Sicard and Clerc, who promoted the use of signs in education, is credited with the early establishment of sign language in American schools for the deaf.[7] Clerc introduced the French educational method at the American School for the Deaf in Hartford, and through his travels in New England with Gallaudet, he fostered the use of sign language in other schools for the deaf, including at the New York Institution for the Instruction of the Deaf and Dumb, which opened in spring of 1820, and the Pennsylvania Institution for the Deaf and Dumb, which opened in the fall of the same year.[8] Soon other states followed their example: the Kentucky Asylum for the Tuition of the Deaf and Dumb opened in 1823, then similar schools in Ohio in 1829 and in Virginia in 1839. Maryland School for the Deaf was the twenty-seventh state school to open, in 1868.[9]

This piece of nineteenth-century history leaves out the more important story of how these institutions were built in the first place. The first schools for the deaf in Hartford, New York City, and Philadelphia were built as part of the same impulse that gave rise to new prisons, hospitals, schools for the blind, and free public schools for poor children.[10] In Philadelphia beginning in 1800, philanthropists and civic leaders began to form societies to study how to handle the city's growth, and the problems that came with an influx of children and adults into the city. Residents in colonial cities like Philadelphia and Hartford complained that they found themselves increasingly living in small, crowded areas alongside "ex-slaves, unemployed immigrants, vagrants, criminals, juvenile delinquents, poverty-stricken derelicts, and a raft of uneducated children," raising the question of how they should respond to the problems facing cities that were growing larger each year.[11] One response was to separate the different classes of individuals—deaf, blind, insane, criminal, and sick—and organize them into separate institutions so that special forms of rehabilitation and education could be applied to them. Like institutions for the blind and asylums for the insane, the first schools for the deaf in the United States were given the same designation, as asylums and institutions to house deaf children.

Not only did city leaders believe that afflicted individuals should be removed from their surroundings; they also believed that the different classes of disabled and deviant should be kept separate from one another. Women and men should be separate, as should petty criminals from more violent criminals.[12] By the same extension, they also believed deaf children should be educated separately from hearing children.

The idea of categorizing and identifying children by a shared physical or mental trait is entirely accepted now, but as David Rothman observes, it was a uniquely nineteenth-century development. Before what he calls the "discovery of the asylum," colonial America had no such plan of segregation for these categories of "infirmities."[13] Deaf children, as were children who were blind, poor, and otherwise disabled, were generally tolerated and allowed to live among their families and neighbors. If education was provided, it was provided individually and according to family ability. When Mason Cogswell's daughter was deafened from scarlet fever at the age of two, he employed a tutor for her, and she continued to live in the household. But when her progress was slow, Cogswell began to explore European approaches.[14] In their rapidly expanding cities, whether Hartford, New York City, or Philadelphia, the city leaders sought a solution for the increasing number of deaf children—as well as blind and poor children—living among them. Michael Ignatieff describes their commitment to institution building as guided by a common belief that there should be a "social distance between the confined and the outside world."[15]

The Pennsylvania Institution for the Deaf and Dumb was established in 1820, three years after the American School for the Deaf was founded in Hartford. It may not have the distinction of being the first school for the deaf in the country, but its early history is equally notable. Through the copious writings of its board of directors, particularly by one of its enthusiastic members, Roberts Vaux, we have an exceptional view into the beliefs and motives of the nineteenth-century designers of education for deaf children in special schools.

The idea of an institution for the deaf was first presented to the citizens of Philadelphia by Thomas H. Gallaudet and Laurent Clerc, who were on a speaking tour on the subject of their newly opened school in Hartford. Speaking in the city on December 7, 1816, they impressed enough individuals that "great interest was aroused" and a committee of leading citizens of the city agreed to meet for the purpose of exploring the possibility of a similar institution in Philadelphia.[16] Because there was reluctance to compete with the school at Hartford, plans were delayed a few years. At the time, David Seixas, a Jewish merchant and inventor who had been dabbling in philosophy, came across the work of the Abbé Sicard, and by his own initiative persuaded a few deaf children he had seen playing in the streets to allow him to try educating them. A small classroom in his home came to the attention of those city leaders who had been contemplating an institution for the deaf, and he was invited to meet with them to discuss those plans.[17]

The philanthropists and leaders who appointed themselves the first board of directors of the Pennsylvania Institution for the Deaf and Dumb were among some of the most prominent and well-known individuals in Philadelphia and throughout the United States. Roberts Vaux, a Quaker and active reformer, was invited to join because at the time he was spearheading efforts to build a public-school system open to all children, including the poor, in the city of Philadelphia. A prolific organizer, Vaux also sat on the boards of the Philadelphia Prisons Society, the Association of Friends for the Instruction of the Poor, and the Pennsylvania Abolition Society.[18] The president of the board was the Reverend William White, who was elected the first bishop of the Episcopalian Church in America. Also on the board was Horace Binney, a Quaker and practicing attorney, who was at one time considered for appointment to the U.S. Supreme Court, but he declined, citing his desire to remain in Philadelphia.[19] Jacob Gratz was a member of a prominent Jewish family in Philadelphia, and as with other members of his family and his colleagues, sat on a number of boards of societies and organizations.[20] Franklin Bache, who later replaced Reverend White as president of the board of directors, was a distinguished physician and an active member of the city's Temperance Society.

Once constituted, the board quickly became involved in the design and planning of the new institution, even though none of them had any personal knowledge of deaf children, or had a relative who was deaf. Instead they were motivated both by philanthropy and the eagerness to participate in the redesign of the city of Philadelphia. In one of the board's first statements, authored by Roberts Vaux and signed by each member of the board, they proclaimed:

> Among the various efforts of Philanthropy and Learning, to enlarge the circle of human happiness and knowledge, none, perhaps, should rank higher than those which have been directed to the discovery and application of means for the instruction of the deaf and

dumb . . . [and we are] Desirous . . . of extending the benefits of instruction, and with it the incomparable solace of rational social intercourse to that portion of our fellow beings who are deprived of the faculties of speech and hearing.[21]

They believed that they were helping deaf children gain an education, but more grandly, they were building, one institution at a time, a massive system to address the changing composition of American society. As board members served on other boards, plans and ideas were exchanged among the different institutions. Roberts Vaux introduced to the school many of the same ideas he had used in designing the public school system in Philadelphia, in particular his fondness for the Lancasterian model of education. Students would be taught in groups and supervised by "monitors" or teachers who would sit at the head of the class, replacing the individual tutorial arrangement that was in place during the colonial period. Because so many children needed to be grouped together in a classroom, strict control of behavior was required to maintain order.[22] Education not only introduced new skills, but it was also, first and foremost, intended to instill a code of moral conduct among children, especially among the poor or immigrants, whose upbringing was considered less than ideal.

Shortly after the school opened, the board decided that providing instruction alone was not sufficient; the children would also need to live at the school so that the totality of the institution's effect could be impressed on them. Deaf children who were wont to run without inhibition in the street would be brought into the institution and taught the proper manner of conduct both in their learning and their social behaviors. As with the plans for building orphanages, prisons, and other institutions, the new school was to command control of the entire body of the child, not only to educate, but also to feed and house—to turn the child into a being of intelligence and proper conduct. A new "asylum" would be erected such that "the pupils may be suitably accommodated, since it is indispensably necessary for the well-ordering of the establishment that the children be more withdrawn from publick intercourse, and that a seperation [sic] of the sexes be more rigidly enforced."[23] Further, on admission, parents or guardians were required to affix their signature to an agreement as follows: "Whereas the Pennsylvania Institution for the Deaf and Dumb has admitted (my son, daughter, or ward, as the case may be) into the asylum, for the purpose of instruction, and has also agreed to educate (or educate, clothe, and maintain, as the case may be) him or her, during the time he or she may remain under its care, free of charge to me, I hereby relinquish him or her to the sole control of the said institution."[24] In a city facing rapid population growth, institutions were seen as a means of managing its unfortunate citizens, in order to repair their condition and instill in them all manner of appropriate behavior.

One of the board's first actions was to appoint David Seixas the new principal of the school. He had become well-known in Philadelphia for his efforts with deaf children, and given his familiarity with the ideas of the Abbé de l'Epée, the directors believed him to be an ideal head for the new school.[25] Even with Seixas at the helm, the directors continued to meet frequently to discuss details of the new institution, from the appointment of teachers, to the design of its buildings, to how the children would be fed and clothed. They wrote frequent directives to Seixas regarding the hours of schooling, the size of the classrooms, and the curricula to be taught.[26] A Women's Committee was constituted to work with the matron who supervised the girls' living quarters.[27] An equally distinguished group of Philadelphia women served on the committee, including Roberts Vaux's wife, Margaret Wistar, also from an active philanthropic family, and Rebecca Gratz, the sister of Jacob Gratz.

Once installed as the head of the board's education committee, Vaux impressed on the directors his ideals for equal education for all, including the poor. The institution would be open to all deaf children, those with the ability to pay tuition and those who were indigent. At first, the school was supported by "subscriptions," or private contributions from wealthy Philadelphia citizens, but the directors soon recognized that private contributions alone would not be sufficient to support the school, and that if they were to hold to the ideal of an education for poor and disabled children, the state would have to be persuaded to contribute regularly to the school's treasury. In January 1821, two board members, accompanied by David Seixas and six of their students, traveled to the Pennsylvania legislature in Harrisburg and after a short presentation, succeeded in convincing the state to begin supporting the institution. For those without the ability to pay, the state would provide $160 per child per annum for a term of schooling not to exceed three years. The school admitted twenty-five students in its first year of operation, and after only one year, enrollment grew so quickly that their original quarters became too small, and the school relocated to another building in the city.[28]

Barely a year after the Pennsylvania Institution for the Deaf and Dumb opened its doors, the board of directors was delivered a shocking accusation. The mother of Letitia Ford, a fourteen-year-old admitted to the school as an indigent, complained to a member of the board that the principal, David Seixas, had been "taking hold of and pinching [her daughter's] thighs, taking her by the nose and ear and pulling them," and then "made her (the daughter) an offer of a dollar and also to give her fine cloths from which she could only believe that he mediated the seduction of her daughter."[29] In just a few years, David Seixas had achieved a not small amount of celebrity and accolades for his work at the school, so the accusation was wholly unexpected. Deciding the complaint was serious, the board appointed a committee of its lawyer members to conduct an investigation.[30]

The committee members approached the matron, Mary Cowgill,

and asked if she had observed any improprieties in the principal's conduct toward his students. She confessed that she had, but had to date been reluctant to inform them. Beginning her account, she explained that "going one morning into the chamber of the girls before breakfast [she] received a complaint from Letitia Ford . . . that David Seixas had during the night just past visited that chamber . . . and particularly had come to the bedside of [another female pupil] Catherine Hartman and herself, placed his hands on the bed and taken hold of her leg, that Catherine Hartman her bedfellow whose foot he had also taken hold of, was excessively alarmed." In response, the matron had the lock on their door repaired, and a bedstead propped against their door.[31]

A few months later, in May of 1821, another student, Eliza Williams, "on coming down stairs to tea from the schoolroom, where she had been detained by the Principal after the dismissal of the class, on account of some misbehavior, appeared greatly agitated and immediately after tea complained with expressions of disgust against David Seixas, of his having kissed her." The matron called in another student who had been with Eliza and claimed the student confirmed the account. Shortly after, despite her precautions to lock their chamber door, the girls again complained to the matron that Seixas was entering their rooms at night without a candle. The cook, whose bed was in the same room as the girls', gave an account: "She soon discovered it was Mr. Seixas from the light of the lamp in the street and its being a clear starlight night, he came in very quietly, was undressed above his waist but she was not sure that he had his pantaloons off, from his silent tread she was sure he had no shoes on—he looked about the chamber and soon left it, closing the door after him very carefully."[32]

The next obvious course of action would be to interview the female pupils to determine if in fact their accounts were consistent with the matron's, but none on the committee or the board could understand the pupils at all. The students signed but the directors did not. They were entirely dependent on the matron for any information from their deaf charges: "Aware of the difficulty that would occur in obtaining testimony from those of the unfortunate pupils of the Institution whom they intended to examine, if dependant [sic] altogether upon their own means of eliciting it from them determined to call in the aid of the matron, whose superior knowledge of the requisite signs would render this part of their duty much more satisfactory themselves as well as to the board." Through the matron, the committee posed questions to Letitia Ford, but she seemed unable to understand all the questions they wanted to ask. "Finding she could not comprehend other questions stated to her recourse was had to signs which by the same means she most expressively showed us that David had visited the girls' chamber at night that he came to the bed of herself and bedfellow Catherine Hartman at night and first placed his hand under the clothes on C. Hartman and then placed it over to her, after which he walked round the foot of the bed and attempted to turn down the clothes which he seized hold of, when he hugged and kissed her."[33]

Brought before the committee and the board to answer these accusations, David Seixas was outraged at the students' "inventive slanders." Yes, he had entered their chambers, but it was for entirely innocent reasons. He had once kissed the hand of Eliza Williams, upon praising her for her good progress in his classroom, but nothing more. But "while she wore a smile on her face, her heart was wrinkled with anger," because she shortly after gave the matron the impression he had gone further. As for his forays into their bedchambers at night, he had noticed on several occasions that they had left their candles burning, at great danger of fire to themselves, so he had entered their rooms to put out the candles. On one occasion, he had opened their door long enough to throw a pint of water inside the rooms to quiet the girls because they had been making noises in their chamber, but under no circumstances had he ever conducted any sort of impropriety toward them, certainly not hugging or kissing them. Seixas was indignant: "Those pupils had been by me generally collected from the alleys and courts of our suburbs, their parentage was lower than humble and obscure and in some cases, it originated in the dregs of society. Already before their entrance into the Asylum, I had fed many, clothed some and instructed all. I had rescued them from a stage of vagrancy, I had raised them to partial habits of mental and physical industry, I beheld them elevated by the labours that resulted from my own personal sacrifices . . . Who cultivates a vegetable— who rears an animal, a brute—and yet feels not a kindred like sensation?" Seixas admitted to no more than an "affectionate vigilance" for his pupils, and was bitterly disappointed to find they had turned against him with "suspicions of criminality."[34]

Upon receiving the report of the investigative committee and Seixas's response, the board began to deliberate whether Seixas should be dismissed from his duties as principal.[35] Immediately the board divided in half. On one side were those who believed Seixas had no cause to enter their bedrooms at night in the first place, and more, that there was enough evidence he may have conducted himself inappropriately with respect to hugging and kissing the girls. On the other side were those who believed Seixas was entirely innocent and had acquitted himself by explaining inconsistencies in the female pupils' accounts of their interactions with him. Seixas argued that after the matron was informed of Letitia Ford's mother's complaints, she began to regard him differently, viewing even innocent actions on his part as potentially perverse.

As the board deliberated in executive session, several motions were made, each failing until a motion to dismiss Seixas only for having improperly entered the girls' chamber at night passed by a narrow margin.[36] The board's decision to release Seixas from his employment drew calls of outrage from the Philadelphia community. Newspapers and pamphlets were published in his defense, and friends rallied to his support. Citing the narrow majority vote, his supporters claimed he had been dismissed on indefensible grounds. Some charged that anti-Semitism had caused his harsh treatment and disregard for his many accomplishments both for the school and for the community at large. As a further show of support, Seixas's friends and sympathizers helped to found a rival institution, the Philadelphia Asylum for the Deaf and Dumb, which lasted only a few years until the state legislature declined to provide funding for the asylum, instead favoring the Pennsylvania Institution for the Deaf and Dumb.[37]

Roberts Vaux complained later in a confidential letter to a friend that he still believed Seixas had committed wrongdoing, and that those on the board who were "showing mercy to Seixas . . . could not do justice to the helpless and exposed beings under his charge."[38] Seixas had undermined public trust in his new institution, and for this Vaux was deeply shaken.[39]

The nineteenth-century institution was a means of education as well as a separately organized *place* of education. It was conceived as a way to remove the afflicted—the deaf, the blind, the insane, and the criminal—"from the streets" where they were wont to wander without constraint, and place them in more regimented environments. As they met to make plans for the school, the directors of the Pennsylvania Institution for the Deaf and Dumb immediately began planning how to raise funds for a new building.

Indeed, Rothman describes reformers of New York and Pennsylvania, including Vaux and his contemporaries, as greatly occupied with the details of the architecture of their institutions—the rooms within, the ways in which the occupants would be separated from one another, and how they would travel between the different parts of the building: "Unlike their predecessors, they turned all their attention inward, to the divisions of time and space within the institution."[40] They viewed the design of buildings as "one of the most important of the *moral* sciences," since it was believed that controlling the movement of bodies within space would be the means by which rehabilitation would be accomplished.

Vaux's ideas for the Pennsylvania Institution for the Deaf and Dumb were borrowed freely from his participation in the planning of other institutions. While serving on the board of the Pennsylvania Institution for the Deaf and Dumb, Vaux was also deeply involved in the planning and design of a new penitentiary for Pennsylvania. Through his research and correspondence with reformers in England and elsewhere in Europe, he devised a plan based on the idea that the best path to rehabilitation was to enforce a rigid physical separation between criminals. While other states proposed enforcing silence and prohibiting communication among criminals, Vaux wanted actual physical separation. Ryon traced Vaux's commitment to this system to his Quaker heritage: "Thoughts of beating and chaining their fellowmen repelled them, and they believed the silent meditations of the meeting house would be matched in penitentiaries where inmates could not disturb one another. They trusted in the power of association, good and bad, and argued that a prisoner who saw and talked only to pious, dedicated visitors chosen by the state or by private organizations would feel their influence."[41]

Vaux's sentiments about the correct treatment of prisoners were not much different than his beliefs about how to educate deaf children. As the directors planned who should be employed in the institution, they sought individuals of "moral deportment . . . benevolent dispositions and a philosophic cast of mind."[42] Education would be carried out in a new building that would separate female and male students, and spaces would be designated within the school for sleeping, eating, and education. Likewise, as with his plans for inmates in the new penitentiary, Vaux insisted that the Pennsylvania Institution for the Deaf and Dumb deem it "absolutely necessary by law to forbid corporal punishment in the asylum." Instead of flogging and other forms of physical abuse, Vaux and his contemporaries conceived of a new future shaped by changed environments—in the design of buildings, in the correct choice of teachers and caretakers, and in the planning of a healthful and moral educational curriculum.[43]

Nineteenth-century institutions for deaf pupils retrieved deaf children from their homes around the city and in neighboring areas, indeed "rescued" them, but once brought to the institution, began to regulate their movements in the interests of education and rehabilitation. Where once deaf children and young adults had lived among their neighbors, working alongside family members and other members of their community, they were now removed from homes and workplaces and brought to new places of association. As they were identified as "deaf and dumb" and brought into the institution, they became "inmates" and objects of study. Shortly after the Pennsylvania Institution for the Deaf and Dumb appointed Seixas as their principal, they also appointed two "respectable" physicians who would attend to their pupils in the school. From the start, as the institution brought children into its care, there began a set of practices designed to name, identify, medically classify, and rehabilitate the deaf pupils.[44]

It is perhaps ironic then that so soon after the school opened its doors and admitted its first class of deaf pupils, there was a scandal over *bodies*. It is hard to determine from the record whether the principal of the school, David Seixas, in fact "indecently" touched the female pupils under his care. Crucially we have no direct report of what the deaf female pupils experienced, except when mediated through the matron and others' accounts of their "pantomime," most of which Seixas vigorously refutes. In his own words, though, Seixas does admit to an "affectionate vigilance" for his students; he admits to kissing their hands and expresses sentiments of "attachment." He did visit their rooms as they slept, though as he says, to be sure their candles were not left burning. He did touch them in their beds, but only to reassure them that he was vigilant in their care.

What could have compelled Seixas to collect the deaf children he saw playing on the streets outside his shop those few years before? Was he drawn to pursue the Enlightenment question of whether a human being exists before language, and before training brings it into being? Did he see in the deaf children the possibility of answering age-old questions about the relationship between the senses and the mind? Or was he drawn to their exoticism, the mesmerizing difference of their gestural language? Did he wonder at their playfulness and liveliness despite the fact that they live without sound? Once he began to care for them in a captive community, did his gaze become more proprietary—and sexualized?

In his classic analysis of prisons and asylums, Foucault describes institutions as creating in those who build them a new power not only to observe, but also to label and regulate the movements of individuals. Because there is an imbalance of power, where caretakers have the power to watch and the patients do not, Foucault describes institutions as channeling the sentiments of caretakers from sensations of power to ones of erotic desire for those who are watched: "They were fixed by a gaze, isolated and animated by the attention they received. Power operated as a mechanism of attraction; it drew out those peculiarities over which it kept watch. Pleasure spread to the power that harried it; power anchored the pleasure it uncovered."[45]

The imbalance of power is deepened by the fact that the watched and the observed do not, indeed, *cannot* speak on their behalf. When the directors of the Pennsylvania Institution for the Deaf and Dumb tried to interview the young women to determine whether in fact Seixas had done the things that were claimed, they found them essentially "dumb," and unable to speak. Although it would have been relatively easy to understand the girls in sign language, their testimonies were filtered through the matron, and thus reduced to hearsay. When the students were deprived of a voice of their own, David Seixas could claim that the directors had misunderstood the young women's pantomime, or that the matron was ill-disposed against Seixas. The most insidious effect of institutions designed in this way, in Foucault's words, is the silencing of those under their care. They are rendered mute. Further deepening their silence was the fact that the women were from poor families whose claim to public charity was fragile and tenuous.

Thus is the conflicting legacy of the nineteenth-century institution: it brought education to deaf children and brought them together in a sign language community, even as it made this community more vulnerable to abuses of power. The first schools for deaf children in the United States were not private or exclusive, but were built with the intention to educate the wealthy and the indigent alike. Many of these schools actively sought out deaf children isolated in remote townships and urged their parents to let them attend school with other deaf children.

Once the students came to the school, a new language community began to develop. The board of directors of the Pennsylvania Institution for the Deaf and Dumb made scant reference to the fact that their pupils were already using sign language at the time they arrived at the school because for them, signing was a given, and its presence in the school was unproblematic.[46] After dismissing David Seixas as principal, they employed Laurent Clerc, the principal of the school for the deaf in Hartford, whose position in support of sign language in the education of deaf children was known to all. The school did not see signing as controversial; indeed the minutes of the board of directors were marked by a general absence of any debate about its presence in the first decades of its founding. The nineteenth-century institution sustained language communities by providing stable access to sign language to generations of young deaf children.

Sign language communities aside, the troubling side of the legacy of the nineteenth-century institution is its design. Foucault describes asylums as organized not only by *silence*—both the oppressive silencing of its "inmates," or pupils, and the reciprocal silence of the caretakers, usually those who are not deaf and do not sign well—but also by what he calls *perpetual judgment,* or the constant reminders to the inmates of the nature of their condition, what he calls "a sort of invisible tribunal in permanent session."[47] Roberts Vaux and his contemporaries conceived of the highly centralized design of institutions as a way for the benevolent and patriarchal caretaker to exert moral principles on those who were afflicted with disability. But as Vaux would discover to his dismay, the highly centralized form of caretaking too easily led to abuse of all types, from sexual to physical and emotional. Vaux believed good intentions could guide institutions, but Foucault argues otherwise: that powerlessness and repression were built directly into the design of the nineteenth-century institution. Their directors failed to observe within themselves the seeds of abuse that come from unchecked power over people unlike themselves.

Sadly, the troubled legacy of the nineteenth-century school for the deaf would persist into the twentieth century. In 2001, the Maine State Legislature authorized the payment of damages to a group of former students at the Maine School for the Deaf who suffered years of physical and sexual abuse. They allege that the school's isolated location on a bucolic island off the eastern coast of Maine, together with indifference from the state and its board of directors, allowed staff members to continue to inflict abuse on their deaf students, even when the children and their parents complained.[48] Other deaf schools have had similar scandals.

Foucault observed in asylums a third principle of power and control. In addition to *silence* and *perpetual judgment,* he explains what he calls *recognition by mirror,* or the act of humiliating inmates by showing them that they are not as extraordinary as they believe because others have the same condition. In a repressive asylum, the effect is to dis-empower inmates by making them feel less unique, reduced in the end to being nothing more than insane. Where the inmate may once have believed in a manic moment that he was royalty, the exaltation is lost when confronted with other inmates who also believe themselves to be the King of France. The inmate discovers the condition (of being manic) and is deflated, or as Foucault says, "would see itself as spectacle."[49]

Paradoxically, the very same quality of recognition, in a humanistic environment, can be used to liberate. This may be what makes schools for the deaf such compelling places. When deaf students arrive at a school for the deaf and see for the first time not only deaf students but also Deaf adults as staff, teachers, and principals, or even superintendents, there is recognition of the self in the other—not necessarily as identical, but as possibles. In more simple terms, deaf children see in others ways of living that they might imagine for themselves. The child no longer feels alone, freakish, or wholly responsible for oneself—no longer royalty perhaps, but finally, human in a community of others. In her autobiography, the French deaf actress Emmanuelle Laborit tells the story of a deaf friend who discovers as a teenager that she is not, as her parents have told her, the only deaf person in the world. Enraged, she confronts her parents and asks why they gave her such a belief; their reply was that "it was for her own good."[50]

Today, nearly all schools for the deaf founded in the nineteenth century have redesigned themselves and shaken off their older appearances. Some, like the Maryland School for the Deaf, have scaled down their institutional architecture and replaced their buildings with more modest structures. The California School for the Deaf moved from its original campus in Berkeley, built in 1868, to another location farther south, using the opportunity to build a new campus with smaller one-story buildings and cottages instead of large dormitories. The Pennsylvania Institution for the Deaf and Dumb moved four times in its history, increasing in size each time until it settled in 1842 on a large plot of land in Mount Airy, a then-rural outpost of Philadelphia.[51] By 1984, however, the school could no longer expect enrollments large enough to justify its outsized campus and the number of large buildings, leading it to sell its campus and move to a smaller former military academy for boys.

Whereas institutions for the deaf once claimed the entire lives of deaf students, housing them for weeks and months at a time, many of them now have sharply reduced or abandoned their residential programs. Either students don't board at all at the school, or they go home at the end of each week if they live too far to commute daily. The common experience of deaf students prior to the 1950s, when they endured long separations from home and family, has vanished. In the twenty-first century, the body of the deaf child now no longer belongs entirely to the school—instead, responsibility for the child is shared by families, school districts, doctors, and other professionals, each competing for the child. Recognizing this, schools for the deaf now "market" themselves as a choice.

When Deaf adults talk about their memories as children, most will remember their years at a school for the deaf. These are memories of lifelong friendships that were formed in the schools, and childhoods spent together in a small community. The memories are sometimes poetic and nostalgic, as when Patrick Graybill recited a poem about watching as a child from his parents' car as they drove the long distance from his small hometown to the Kansas School for the Deaf in Olathe. As the car approached the school, he would begin to see the water tower, marking the spot of the school underneath, drawing him close to a community of friends and Deaf adults whom he remembers as having a deep and positive influence on his life. Some will talk of images of separation. Bernard Bragg tells of the emotional moment when his mother brought him to Fanwood, the New York School for the Deaf, to begin school for the first time, and then after a kiss at the doorstep, she turned and quickly left him. Ted Supalla remembers an unexpected moment when a hearing child from the neighborhood outside the school unwittingly rode a bicycle across the campus of the Washington School for the Deaf. Through a simple act, he had pierced the school's boundaries and violated the segregation of deaf children inside the school from those hearing children living outside. Some schools for the deaf to this day have iron fences and gates, a holdover from a time when the boundaries were clear and crossing them was imagined to be dangerous.

Older deaf people recall a world where the choice was either to go to a school for the deaf, or remain home alone and isolated. Deaf men and women born during the first half of the twentieth century remember a time when all their friends graduated from a school for the deaf, so to ask where someone is "from" is to ask which school they attended, not where they were born. Younger deaf people talk about schools for the deaf as places of self-discovery. When a Deaf acquaintance was a teenager, she demanded that her parents enroll her in a school for the deaf because she had grown tired of navigating the social and psychological demands of a high school with hearing students, and she wanted to explore being deaf with other deaf teenagers.

In recent years when desegregation of public schools has been so hard fought, it seems odd to choose to be separate, but for many deaf children and their families, the choice is a conscious one, made despite a wariness about institutions and segregation. At schools for the deaf, Deaf students can sign with their principals and the office secretary. They can be tutored by the teacher's aide, and sign up for wrestling with a Deaf coach. Their teachers are often Deaf and were themselves educated at a school for the deaf, which allows them to offer shared experiences with students. Indeed, this is the most compelling characteristic of schools for the deaf: They offer education and community in sign language, and create for their students possibilities of social interaction that would otherwise be difficult or strained in a hearing school. In their "apart-ness," schools for the deaf offer safe harbor for deaf students who find being alone—or with a small group of other deaf peers immersed among hearing people—too difficult to endure.

Schools for the deaf in the twenty-first century carry within their walls and inside their fences the legacy of an older time. Buildings have been demolished or entirely redesigned, in hopes that new spaces may lead schools to be more humane places. The boundaries of the school have become more flexible and porous. No longer are deaf children separated so severely from their families. There are experiments with educating deaf children both inside and outside school walls—as in the case of deaf children who spend half their day at a public school and return to the deaf school in the afternoons. In another experiment, the city of New York converted P.S. 47, a former public school for deaf children, into a bilingual school that also admits hearing children who use ASL (either because their parents are deaf, or they have learned ASL as a second language). The school carries out the ideal of education in a language community but does not segregate deaf children. These are tantalizing experiments because they try to reconcile the benefits of schools for deaf children with the ideals of integration. Deaf people firmly believe in the power of education to save deaf children, so the question lingers: How can deaf children be educated within a community, as Deaf people wish, without falling into the trap of the nineteenth-century asylum where their bodies are managed and rendered powerless? The answer seems almost at hand, but it requires imagination for a new generation of deaf children.

2
An Entirely Separate School

Just beyond the main building of the South Carolina School for the Deaf and the Blind, toward the edge of campus, there is a gently rising spot of land with low-hanging trees and a fence around it. It is the Cedar Springs Baptist Church cemetery. Once adjacent to the old Presbyterian church farther down the hill, the cemetery over the years became surrounded by classroom buildings. In existence when the school opened in 1849, the old family cemetery has aged tombstones leaning to the side with faded carvings.

Buried in the cemetery is the founder and first superintendent of the South Carolina Institution for the Deaf, Dumb and the Blind, Newton Pinckney Walker, who died suddenly from the measles in 1861, leaving his wife briefly in charge of the school. Soon after, their son returned from serving in the Civil War and took over his father's position. Upon his death some fifty years later, he too was buried in the cemetery.[1] For generations of families who lived in nearby Spartanburg, as well as devoted teachers and directors of the school, the cemetery was their final resting place.

Behind the rows of family tombstones is a less adorned section, where instead of gently hanging trees, the land is open and dotted with short bushes. This is the African-American section of the cemetery, where there lie mostly river rocks and temporary funeral markers where the handwritten names of the deceased have faded. A few modest tombstones stand in this section; one marks the burial spot of Jones Ed Mills, a laborer at the school who drove a mule-drawn wagon to nearby Cedar Springs each day to pick up and deliver the mail. On his tombstone reads, "In remembrance of his faithful and love to the children at S.C.D. & B." Though there are no markers, African-American deaf students were almost certainly buried here, along with other African-American residents of Cedar Springs.

The two sides of the cemetery stand as a lingering reminder that for most of their early history, schools for deaf children in the South taught their white and African-American children separately. From the middle of the nineteenth century until desegregation began in 1955, every school for the deaf in the southern states made "separate" arrangements based on race. Almost every southern state and the District of Columbia had separate campuses for Black deaf students; the rest, like Arkansas and South Carolina, had separate buildings on the same campus. In 1870, the State of Tennessee bought land adjacent to the school for the deaf for the express purpose of housing a new department; the land came with a former house, and some farm buildings, which were renovated to support a school for fifty African-American deaf children. At first, Kendall School for the Deaf at Gallaudet University did not separate children based on race. In 1906, however, the U.S. Congress, in its capacity as oversight government of the District of Columbia, changed policy and directed the D.C. Board of Education to send African-American deaf children out of state to Baltimore at the Institute for the Colored Blind, which opened a new department for Black deaf children.[2]

The practice of segregating by race and gender in deaf schools was followed a few years later with another type of segregation. As the oral method began to gain currency in American deaf education toward the end of the nineteenth century, schools began to place deaf children in different classrooms based on the type of educational method to be used with them, that is, whether their teachers should sign (the "manual method") or should only speak (the "oral method"). From the earliest days of deaf education, the bodies of deaf children have been organized in different kinds of schemes, from segregation by gender, to race, to separation by educational method. Today segregation by race is illegal in American schools, but some schools still separate deaf children—by keeping children with cochlear implants in classrooms apart from other deaf children.

Through the nineteenth century, it was common practice in many schools for the deaf to arrange for the burial of children who had died while under the care of the school. The school had already taken over all needs of the child, from buying cloth for clothing, supplying leather for shoes, and providing meals and board at the school as well as medical care. Taking care of the body after death was a natural extension of the school's responsibility. The Kansas School for the Deaf has a cemetery across the street and down the road. Students as well as teachers from the American School for the Deaf are buried in a cemetery not far from the original site of the school.[3] In the nineteenth century, students who died while at school were often simply interred in nearby cemeteries.

In July 1863, Elizabeth Gordon, a student at the South Carolina Institution for the Deaf, Dumb and the Blind, fell ill to "inflammatory rheumatism." By October, she had succumbed. Instead of returning her body to her family, most likely because Charleston was two days' ride from Spartanburg, she was buried in the cemetery. Note was made of her death in the school's annual report: "An honored member of your Board conducted the burial service and, followed by her silent and sightless companions, who deeply lament her loss, her remains were deposited in the cemetery attached to the grounds of the institution. Though this child had been under instruction but a few months, she gave, during her illness, pleasing evidences that she had obtained at least some conceptions of spiritual things; for but a short time prior to her death, she pointed with her palsied and attenuated hands to the skies, saying, in signs, that she was going thither after death."[4]

If Elizabeth Gordon's remains were marked with a tombstone, it no longer exists, nor does a tombstone remain for James Brown, an African-American deaf student who was killed in 1888 while walking along a railroad track.[5] The school's annual reports until the beginning of the twentieth century refer to deaf and blind children who died while at the school, and some, it can be surmised, were buried at the Cedar Springs cemetery.

As schools extended their command over the bodies of their students, they began to determine how these bodies should be organized within the school. The segregation of white and African-American deaf children lasted over one hundred years, from 1867 when North Carolina established a separate Deaf and Dumb Asylum for the Colored until the last such deaf school closed in Baton Rouge, Louisiana, in 1978. Segregating deaf children was official policy enacted by school directors and boards, a course of action that would put into motion different histories for African-American and white Deaf people in the United States. As in the rest of society at that time, African-American Deaf men and women often could not get the same jobs as white Deaf men and women. Deaf clubs were segregated; along with white Deaf clubs, where Deaf people associated in the evenings and weekends away from work, there were Black Deaf clubs sometimes only a few blocks away.[6] The Union League, a large and powerful Deaf club in New York City, aggressively sought out African-American Deaf athletes for its basketball team, but none were permitted to join as members. The separation was so complete for such a long period of time that to this day, many white Deaf people do not know where the Black

Deaf clubs were in their home cities, nor where their members worked and lived, nor do they know very much about the history of deaf schools for African Americans.

The history of separate schools is one of lost histories. Though the *American Annals of the Deaf and Dumb* regularly maintained a census of schools for the deaf, Black deaf schools or "departments" were irregularly listed, often not at all.[7] A combination of shame, fear, neglect, and ignorance have led to a massive loss of historical records from this period. When the Black schools closed, many records were destroyed in a rush to end the final chapter of their histories. As segregation ended, African-American deaf students were moved to white campuses, but never were white students moved to a Black campus. In the transition, many African-American teachers did not move with their students, usually because there were no jobs for them in the newly integrated schools, which meant that much of the oral history of these schools was left behind.[8] Today it is hard to find out very much about the first African-American deaf students who came to the southern schools for the deaf. We know little about who they were, how they arrived at the school, or how they spent their days at the school. Most of what remains today are delicate strands of oral histories, but even these are slowly disappearing as more of the older generation of African-American Deaf students are lost to us.

Some Black deaf schools report informal histories describing how parents of deaf children approached a teacher or a superintendent at a white school, asking for education for their deaf child, but rarely do we know who they were. The founder of the Virginia School for the Colored Deaf and Blind was a white Deaf man, William C. Ritter, who had been a teacher at the Virginia School for the Deaf in Staunton. It is said that he petitioned the state to open a separate school because a mother approached him and asked him to teach her deaf child in exchange for "doing the family washing." As a result of this encounter, he devoted the rest of his life to the education of African-American deaf children in his state.[9] But the names of the mother and her child have disappeared. Unlike the famous first deaf student at the American School for the Deaf at Hartford, whom we know as Alice, the daughter of Mason Cogswell, we can find no memory of the first African-American deaf children in either of these schools. The lingering effect of segregation on deaf education is that the history of the American Deaf community is a splintered one, just barely held together by the lives of African-American and white Deaf people, who share a common sign language and the experience of living as Deaf people in the same country.

In the years immediately after the Civil War, when the country struggled to reunite, there were moments of tantalizing possibility, of opportunities for a different history—where African-American and white deaf children could grow up together in the same schools. But as the stories of Kendall School in Washington, D.C., and South Carolina show, the forces of segregation and racism were far too great to overcome.

A massive enfranchisement of African-American voters in South Carolina after the Civil War ended brought into power the largest number of African-American state representatives and senators in the state's history. In the euphoria of reform and the energy of its new representatives, the government struggled mightily with the difficult task of rebuilding its government and economy.[10] A new state superintendent of education, Justus K. Jillson, was appointed and charged with the responsibility of executing the goals of his party—to bring equality and education to the emancipated African-American citizens in the state. In September 1873, Jillson wrote to the South Carolina School that he had approved applications for three African-American deaf students to enroll there.[11] As state superintendent, he also held a seat on the board of commissioners of the South Carolina Institution for the Education of the Deaf and the Blind, and it was in this capacity that he wrote to Newton Farmer Walker, who had just replaced his father as superintendent of the school. When Walker did not act, he wrote a second time to request that the school admit African-American students who had been "approved by the proper authorities here." Jillson knew that Walker opposed the Republican party and its ideals, so he pressed on: He told Walker that he had to not only admit the students, but also put into practice the principle of equal and *not* separate education for deaf children. His letter to Walker stands today as an early expression of the ideal of integration, one that would not become law until eighty years later, when the Supreme Court ruled in 1954 that separate education was unconstitutional.

> I write in behalf of the board of Comm'rs of the Deaf and Dumb and the Blind to state that the following points relative to the admission of colored pupils into the institution now under your supervision will be strictly and rigidly insisted upon:
>
> 1. Colored pupils must not only be admitted into the institution upon application but an earnest and faithful effort must be made to induce such pupils to apply for admission.
>
> 2. Such pupils, when admitted must be domiciled in the same building, eat at the same table, must be taught in the same classrooms, and by the same teachers and must receive the same attention, care, and consideration as white pupils.[12]

By the end of September 1873, Walker and each of his teachers wrote letters to Jillson announcing that they would resign their positions. Acknowledging their resignations, Jillson required that Walker turn over all accounting books related to the operation of the school to his office in Columbia, an act that effectively closed down the school.[13] But Jillson and his party's control of the South Carolina government was brief: Within three years, Jillson's party was defeated in elections, and he was forced from office.

For a brief moment following the Civil War, the Republican-led legislature in South Carolina fought to enact a new state constitution that would guarantee the rights of African-American voters, create an equal public education system, and bring labor rights to newly emancipated slaves. The constitutional effort would have guaranteed integrated education for African-American and white deaf children, but despite this attempt, the legislature's brief successes would be undone by what South Carolina historian Walter Edgar called an "unrelenting nine-year war to overthrow the Reconstruction regime."[14] Another historian of the South, James Underwood, aptly describes the efforts of Jillson and the Republicans as the "first Reconstruction," which would succeed in granting African-American men the right to vote, but would fail in nearly all other respects. It would take a "second Reconstruction," or the civil rights battles of the 1950s and 1960s, to finally bring about equal education, protection of voting rights, and equal treatment of Black citizens under the law.[15]

With the Republicans overthrown and Democratic rule restored in South Carolina, the South Carolina School reopened in 1879, and Newton F. Walker and his staff were reappointed by the newly installed board of commissioners.[16] The board decreed the school as operating under the same provisions as before, and decided that no African-American deaf children could be admitted until the state provided additional funds to support them. In 1883, funds were finally authorized, and the school opened its first class of African-American deaf children. Jessie Anderson, Jr., the son of a former slave, was one of the first to enroll.[17] He had lost his hearing at age three from meningitis, and at that time had been living with his family in Newberry, about fifty-five miles east of Spartanburg. Jessie came to the South Carolina School at age nine, and remained three years until he left in 1886. For Jessie and the other African-American deaf students, the board designated "the wooden building known as the old hotel situated near to the spring be set apart for the use and occupation of colored deaf and dumb and blind pupils."[18]

The old hotel, dating from before the Cedar Springs property was purchased for a school, was decrepit and barely suitable for habitation, but its main quality was that it was at a distance from the main building. Though the old hotel and the grand main hall were only about two hundred feet apart, there was a thick grove of trees separating them, shielding them from each other. Walker sought to reassure the legislature that he had indeed carried out the wishes of the new government and that his colored department was appropriately segregated, because it "occupies a house some distance from the main building, and although, under the same general management, is an entirely separate school."[19]

As the twentieth century approached, segregation became enacted in public institutions. Deaf schools joined the practice and began to put into place a complicated system of classification that would divide deaf children into multiple categories of distinction. The South Carolina School had already had two categories of students, the deaf and the blind. Walker found shortly after he opened his new school that he was receiving applications from parents of blind students. He knew he could persuade the state to provide funding for blind students as well as deaf if he represented both as a category of children suffering from sensory loss, and the school as an institution responsible for the pitiable and afflicted. Indeed, he was successful, as were superintendents in many other states; many schools had both deaf and blind departments. With his budget augmented, Walker hired a new teacher and bought equipment and books for the blind.[20]

Despite being housed on the same campus, the blind and deaf children were always separate from the start: Deaf students were taught in sign language and blind students were taught music. At South Carolina, as at other schools for the deaf and the blind, teachers of the different departments were either dedicated to music or to speech training and sign language, but never did they teach in both departments. Blind students were never taught sign language even though there was the possibility of teaching them a tactile sign language. For the most part, the two groups could not communicate with each other.

The introduction of race expanded the classification scheme. Geoffrey Bowker and Susan Leigh Star describe the practice of classification as not merely forming abstract semantic distinctions, but as *materially* enacted, a "spatial, temporal or spatio-temporal segmentation of the world."[21] When African-American children enrolled at the South Carolina School for the Deaf and the Blind, the categories of race needed to be mapped onto the existing structure of two separate departments for the different disabilities, deaf and blind. Since deaf and blind students were already housed in different wings of the main building, race had to be added to the existing spatialized scheme. The solution was to further subdivide the school into *four* separate categories, or "departments": two for African-American and white *deaf* children, and two for African-American and white *blind* children. To match the new physical arrangements, new teachers were hired for each department, for the African-American deaf and African-American blind departments, and separate classrooms and sleeping and eating quarters were designated as well.

As can be imagined, maintaining the system quickly grew costly. Over the next years, Walker would submit repeated requests for more funds: "To the casual observer our corps of teachers and officers may appear large for the number of pupils in attendance but it must be remembered that we not only have two separate and distinct departments of the deaf . . . and the blind, respectively, but two subdivisions of these, one for the whites and one for the colored, thus giving us four distinct schools under one general management."[22]

The state legislature, grappling with a depressed state economy, balked at giving more funds to the school until 1900, when it finally appropriated funds for a new building for the "colored" department. By then, the African-American deaf students were living in a building that Walker complained was "unsightly, insecure and very dangerous . . . a very old wooden structure . . . lighted by lamps and candles," unlike the comparatively better furnished main building for white students, which had recently been installed with electricity.[23]

Racializing deafness (and blindness), or institutionalizing distinctions based on race, within an already small population of children, was to institute a crippling legacy of economic and social inequity. Deaf children already segregated in asylums and institutions would be further segregated from within, creating categories, each with different standards. At the South Carolina School, white students lived in a new building, but the African-American deaf students lived in older, decrepit quarters without electricity. Mr. Boney, a teacher in the Black department in South Carolina in 1890, was paid $180 yearly salary, but Miss Ballard, a teacher of articulation in the white department, was paid significantly more at $500 a year.[24] And though they lived on a school campus, African-American deaf students often did manual labor, driving mules and working on the small farm nearby, while white students were relieved of these responsibilities.[25]

In addition to race and sensory condition, many schools for the deaf in the late nineteenth century introduced yet another category, separating signing Deaf children from those who were taught in the "oral" method, or the exclusive use of speech training. Though there had been seeds of the oral movement in deaf schools earlier in the nineteenth century, it did not become an organized and visible movement until the 1870s and 1880s, when proponents of the method gained greater influence.[26] In 1820 when the Pennsylvania Institution for the Deaf and Dumb opened its doors, use of sign language by its students and teachers was accepted as a primary mode of instruction, but by the turn of the century, the same school had changed course and revised the school's teaching methods in favor of the oral approach.[27] Oralists, as they came to be called at the time, had a strong weapon in their arsenal: the highly visible and vocal advocate Alexander Graham Bell, who took on deaf education as a personal cause, in part because he had a deaf mother and a deaf wife. Bell argued that the manual approach was "backwards," and harkened to a primitive age where humans used gesture and pantomime. He believed that teaching speech to deaf students would free them from the confinement of their limited worlds, and enable them to move more freely among hearing people.[28]

For reasons that Douglas Baynton argues had a great deal to do with a fascination with scientific methods and rational practices, the oral philosophy spread quickly to deaf schools throughout the country. Schools increasingly replaced their older teachers with staff whose training was focused more on scientific and rational approaches to education. School curricula turned more to training methods of different types, with speech-reading and lipreading added to vocational education. By the end of the century, the oral movement would overtake most schools for the deaf in the country, with nearly 40 percent of all deaf students reported to be educated in the oral method. By 1920, the number increased even more dramatically to 80 percent.[29] In his annual plea for funds to the South Carolina state legislature in 1890, Newton Farmer Walker added that he was obligated to support not only four "distinct schools under one management," but also "two subdivisions, oral and manual."[30]

By 1881, the superintendent of the Pennsylvania School for the Deaf, A. L. E. Crouter, became convinced that separation of students by teaching method led to better results. Learning to speak required complete devotion and absence of distraction from sign language. If the school tried to keep signing students separate from oral students, Crouter believed, speaking students could focus on the task at hand and perform better.[31]

If the legacy of the early nineteenth century was the establishment of the centralized asylum, the legacy of the *late* nineteenth century was the proliferation of distinctions and segregations within the asylum: first by gender, then by race and language. When the Pennsylvania Institution for the Deaf and Dumb moved to a new campus in the Philadelphia suburb of Mount Airy in 1892, the opportunity was taken to redesign the organization of the school: "The requirements to be met were, therefore, first, a general division of the two systems of teaching (oral / manual); secondly, a separation of the younger from the older pupils; thirdly, in each of these sections, a division by sex, and finally, in each of these resultant parts, a still further division into small groups and families to facilitate supervision." To carry out their goal, the Pennsylvania Institution for the Deaf and Dumb "decided to erect four department buildings . . . the advanced, intermediate, primary and oral departments, each complete in itself, with its own dining-rooms, dormitories, assembly rooms, play grounds, etc., and with its own school-house in the rear."[32]

Like the Pennsylvania Institution for the Deaf and Dumb, many schools reorganized their campuses to accommodate the growing popularity of the oral method, but the reality was that the deaf students often defeated the best efforts of their teachers. In some schools the separation was hard to enforce, because students in the oral and manual departments interacted with each other in spaces away from the classroom, and in the hours after school ended. Playgrounds, dormitories, and dining halls were sometimes as closely supervised as classrooms, but many times not. Despite the best efforts of school administrators, sign language continued to be used, often furtively, among students, and even among some teachers with their students.

But there were places where the separation was total, as in the case of "purely oral" schools such as the Clarke School founded in Northampton, Massachusetts, in 1867, where use of sign language was prohibited throughout school grounds. No doubt the oral movement had a deep effect on the geography of American Sign Language at the beginning of the twentieth century, with some deaf children able to associate with deaf children in other schools through use of sign language, while others were kept entirely isolated from sign language. It should be recognized that separations by educational philosophy did not divide deaf people from one another as deeply and as insidiously as did race. Students in oral and signing departments could, and often did, seek out each other outside the restrictions of the classrooms, but racism kept white and African-American deaf children more completely apart.

A white Deaf student who graduated from the South Carolina School in 1954 remembers that while there, she almost never spoke to the African-American Deaf students because she kept herself strictly separate from them. At this and other deaf schools throughout the South, there were separate dormitories, different teachers and administrators, even separate graduation ceremonies. Sick children did not visit the same infirmary; there was a separate Black infirmary. Their movements on campus through the day followed different paths. She remembers the grove of trees separating the white and Black sections of campus as a dark curtain through which she was afraid to travel.

When M. J. Bienvenu, a graduate of the Louisiana School for the Deaf in Baton Rouge, first met Joe Sarpy, an acclaimed actor in the National Theatre of the Deaf, she discovered to her surprise that he too had graduated from the Louisiana School for the Deaf the same year she did in 1970, yet she did not know him. He was a graduate of the Black deaf school across town, the Louisiana School for the Colored Deaf and Blind. Her school played sports against every other white school for the deaf in the South, but never once against the Black deaf school in the same city.

When a full history is written of Black deaf schools, the story of the different schools will be enriched with detail. Not all Black schools for the deaf were alike. While some schools subdivided their campus as did South Carolina and Arkansas, other schools moved the African-American deaf students to a different campus.

When the North Carolina School for the Deaf in Raleigh found itself receiving applications to admit African-American deaf children, the directors of the school decided they would look for separate quarters for the children before accepting them. They petitioned to the Freedman's Bureau but received only a commitment to improve a building in addition to some support for students. Two years later, in 1869, the state agreed to fund a separate Black deaf department, and nearly thirty students were admitted.[33] A few years later, the state appropriated funds to move the white deaf children to a separate campus in Morganton, North Carolina, some two hundred miles west.[34] Thus North Carolina joined West Virginia; Washington, D.C.; Maryland; Louisiana; Virginia; Alabama; Florida; Georgia; Kentucky; Mississippi; North Carolina; Tenessee; and Texas in having "dual," entirely separate, campuses for African-American and white deaf children.

Ernest Hairston attended a separate campus in West Virginia. Deafened from spinal meningitis at the age of five-and-a-half, Ernest's mother heard about the West Virginia Institute for the Colored Deaf and Blind from a relative, and enrolled her son there. When he arrived in 1946 at the age of seven, there were about 150 students, mostly deaf with a smaller blind department. He remembers not being especially homesick at his new school because he quickly made friends—indeed, more friends than he had had in his small hometown. Located near Charleston, the institute was adjacent to an African-American college, West Virginia State College, and during his years there, he would be educated by African-American teachers who had been trained at the college. His vocational training in barbering and tailoring were taught by men who owned shops in Charleston. The mornings were devoted to academic training, and in the afternoons, the boys took up barbering, upholstery, tailoring, "pressing" (drycleaning), or shoe repair. The girls took beauty culture, cooking, sewing, pressing, or typing. Barbering was favored by boys, who liked the idea of the relative independence of owning one's own barber shop. Specially skilled boys could work in the upholstery department at West Virginia State College. In this sense, the Black deaf school was very much a part of the African-American community of Charleston, a quality Hairston feels made this Black deaf school different from others.[35]

Hairston remembers that the houseparents and teachers lived in the students' dormitory, in rooms between the girls' and the boys' wing of the building. In her memoir about growing up African-American and deaf in the South, Mary Herring Wright remembers with fondness the teachers and school principals who lived on campus with the students at the North Carolina School for the Colored Deaf and Blind at Raleigh. She also remembers many interactions between deaf and blind students on the campus, as does Hairston who credits a partially blind student with teaching him the alphabet when he first arrived at the West Virginia School.[36] It would seem that in some Black deaf schools, the separation between blind and deaf students was not as yawningly wide as it was on some white school campuses. Baynton also finds that Black deaf schools were more likely to be manual schools, and the oral philosophy was not enforced as strictly as it was in many white deaf schools.[37] As the stories of different schools come together, we can start to assemble a composite history of deaf children that acknowledges the effects of classification by race and language.

The end to segregated schools for deaf children came slowly and unevenly. After the Supreme Court ruled in *Brown v. Board of Education* (1954) that separate education for African-American children was discriminatory and unconstitutional, only a few separate schools closed immediately. Most schools took longer to integrate. The West Virginia School was one of the first to comply and closed its doors just one year later, in 1955.[38] Hairston and his classmates moved to the white school campus in Romney as he started high school. Many African-American teachers at his school did not move with the students; some because they had homes and family in Charleston and did not want to relocate, but others because the school at Romney did not have jobs for them. In his history of the integration of the North Carolina schools for the deaf, the former principal of the Black school in Raleigh writes with some lingering bitterness about the year his school closed in 1971, when it "was only a shell of what once had been. Integration had arrived, and we were benefiting, but segregation on a local level was still alive and well, and had been its usual pattern, continuing to disrupt and damage human lives, both Black and White."[39] Invariably, Black schools were the ones to close in the move toward integration; African-American students and their teachers were relocated to white schools, but never white students to Black campuses. As African-American students moved to their new schools or departments, their teachers and principals lost much of their former status and, more often, their jobs.

In 1952, after a long legal battle, the parents of African-American deaf students in the District of Columbia successfully won an order to force Kendall School on the Gallaudet campus to admit their children instead of sending them to Baltimore to the Maryland Institute.[40] Predating the *Brown v. Board of Education* ruling of 1954, this decision did not specifically address segregated education, only that each state and the District of Columbia were obligated to educate children within their boundaries. The parents were within their rights to insist that as residents of the District of Columbia, their children should be educated there. At first Gallaudet resisted admitting the students, claiming that "no facilities were available on campus for them," and that there were "no qualified Negro teachers to teach them."[41] Under pressure, Kendall School admitted the African-American students but housed them in a separate building, an old gym. The students had little interaction with white students, traveling to and from campus not in a school bus with other students, but on contract with Yellow Cab. In a chronicle of the struggle to integrate, the former teachers of the "Division 2," or the Black department of Kendall School, describe how their teaching facilities were clearly less ideal, and how the administration's efforts to keep African-American deaf children, their teachers, and their families separate from the white department continued even after the African-American deaf students were admitted to Kendall.[42]

After the West Virginia School for the Colored Deaf and Blind closed in 1955, other schools followed suit, but some states maintained separate departments and campuses until as late as 1978, when the Louisiana School for the Colored Deaf and Blind finally closed in Baton Rouge. Former students at the West Virginia School for the Colored Deaf and Blind were mailed a letter explaining that the school's records were about to be destroyed, and they had a final opportunity to ask for their own records. But few responded; it seemed inconsequential to ask for one's records from so long ago. Individually, the records tell a story; together they would tell a richer story, but they are mostly gone. The former superintendent of the white campus in Baton Rouge remembers that after the schools were integrated, the remaining records of the Black school were packed into a single trunk and shipped to the white campus—signifying a melancholy ending to this chapter of history.

There are lingering lessons to be learned from the history of white and Black deaf schools, the most important of which is the deep influence that political forces in the larger society can impose on minority cultures. First, in the case of Deaf people, the effects of one hundred years of segregation were broad and deep. Even as white deaf children did not always receive the education they deserved, African-American deaf children in many cases received an even more inferior education. Segregation of deaf children by race as well as from hearing children led to unequal education. Furthermore, the social inequities persisted after deaf children left school.

Deaf clubs, which grew in number and prominence at the turn of the twentieth century, often enforced strict segregation; African-American Deaf men and women could not become members of white clubs. Informal networks of friends and associates were also separate: white Deaf men helped each other get jobs when they heard of openings at the Goodyear Aircraft Company in Akron, Ohio, but they did not extend the same network to African-American Deaf men.

Second, the imposition of categories (deaf, hard of hearing, oral, manual, Black, white) separated deaf children into overly small communities, dramatically increasing the cost of educating them. In the late nineteenth century, segregation was seen as a solution to the problem of deafness and race. It is now against the law to segregate African-American and white children, but the practice of separating deaf children on the basis of other characteristics continues today. In some public schools, parents who want their deaf children educated orally can insist that they attend classrooms separate from Deaf children who sign. Some schools will likewise honor requests by parents of children with cochlear implants to educate their children separately so that they can receive specialized training in speech without interference from sign language.

The impulse to segregate deaf children from one another by some dimension—oral versus total communication, signing versus implanted—is a stubbornly persistent one. And in the twenty-first century as in the nineteenth century, making educational divisions based on category is expensive. Public schools that subdivide deaf children into smaller groups must find space and funding for each different program, from "total communication," which permits signing, to cochlear implant classrooms, which emphasize speaking, increasing the overall cost of educating them and running the real risk that some will be inadequately funded.

Today African-American and white Deaf people are members of the same professional organizations; oral and signing Deaf people who once attended different schools and programs as children now meet together on common ground as adults. Even today, deaf children who attend separate classrooms in public schools still find each other on the playground, or socialize after school. The separations are, on one level, artificial and difficult to enforce once children are adults. Yet such separations create deeply conflicted histories across different groups of Deaf people.

In recent years, Deaf people of various ethnicities have brought their cultures to the American Deaf community. Deaf people of Mexican heritage often maintain their bilingualism in ASL and Mexican Sign Language and travel frequently across both sides of the border, viewing themselves not only as multilingual (they know written Spanish and English), but multicultural as well. In southern California, Deaf churches are attended by recent immigrants from Asia as well as Mexico, and though services are held in ASL, members of the congregation converse among themselves using multiple sign languages. True, the Deaf community grows more diverse, but its diversity is still managed: While there is no longer segregation by ethnicity or race, there are still other kinds of segregations that are permitted, such as by educational philosophy or language preference. Even in the highly contested area of bilingual education, no one would propose that children from Spanish-speaking families be prevented from hearing or using Spanish while at school in order to teach them English, but the practice of preventing deaf children from seeing or using sign language is permitted, even encouraged, by some educators who believe there is no other effective way to teach them to speak English.

The reason why deaf children are treated so severely must be related to their long history as bodies under the control of institutions. This history of deaf children being entirely and completely assigned to institutions, from the time they are admitted as students to the time they die and are buried in cemeteries within the walls of the institution, must represent an enduring belief that deaf childrens' bodies do not belong to anyone but their caretakers.

3

The Problem of Voice

Some of the very first films made in America featured an elephant, two men eating pies, Italians eating macaroni—and a Deaf woman reciting the "Star Spangled Banner" in sign language. Dated 1902, the signing film was among a collection of short segments made by Thomas Edison to demonstrate the potential of "moving picture films."[1] Previously, film could only be viewed through a peephole device, or "kinetoscope," which had among its drawbacks the limitation that only one person could view the film at a time. By 1896, a projection-type device called a "vitascope" was developed that allowed moving picture images to be displayed onto a screen, widening the audience for Edison's new medium. It is easy to imagine why Edison chose a Deaf woman as one of his first subjects for projected images. Through sign language, Edison could show the potential of film to communicate and to show the body and hands in movement. The vitascope was immediately successful and within a year, over a hundred such projectors were in use throughout the country, featuring films for information and entertainment.[2]

A scarce ten years after the invention of cinema, the National Association of the Deaf (NAD) undertook to make "moving picture films" of their own that would be used to advance the goals of the organization, to promote sign language, and to spread the voice of

57

Deaf people throughout the United States and around the world. By 1913, the NAD had made eighteen films.[3] Not all of these films have survived; at least two are believed to be lost. But what remains is a remarkable set of images, not only of what sign language looked like at the turn of the century, but also of what Deaf people wanted—with much urgency—to say to each other and to others. The films ranged in length from as short as 125 feet to about 400 feet, running on the average about eight to nine minutes each. Many have suffered damage, no doubt because they were widely circulated throughout the United States, shipped from one location to another, and shown in halls and auditoriums from North Dakota to New York to California. Some films were damaged due to poor handling by inexperienced film projectionists, with repair often attempted by the Deaf people who rented the films. That so many have survived, and that they remain vivid after so many years, is a story in itself about the surprising durability of early film technology.

The enduring story of these films is the earnest efforts of the "Moving Picture Committee," members of the National Association of the Deaf, to create films that would show that Deaf people have something to say and that they could say it in their own language. The committee debated among themselves about what and who should be the subjects of this costly endeavor, since they were limited to a fund of about $5,000 (about $88,000 dollars today).[4] Some of the films are recitations of poetry and popularly known stories, but others are original texts.

The films reveal the struggle of "voice" at the turn of the century, how Deaf leaders envisioned communicating to Deaf people and to others, and what they would say. "Voice" has dual meaning, most obviously as the modality of expression in spoken language, but also as *being heard*. Without voice, one is mute and inexpressive, and crucially not heard. At the turn of the century, as more schools for the deaf turned to oral education, Deaf people struggled to make themselves heard above the clamor of the demand for speech and the banishment of sign language. The problem of voice facing Deaf people at the time was how to be heard on their own terms.

The years 1911–1913 were pivotal for the oral movement. In 1911, advocates of the speech-only movement had succeeded in persuading the Nebraska state legislature to require the oral method for all students admitted to the Nebraska School for the Deaf. Alarmed that the Nebraska example could spread to other states, the NAD campaigned hard to overturn the bill, failing to do so in 1913 and again in 1915.[5] The NAD believed it had failed because it was up against powerful oral advocates, especially wealthy individuals like Alexander Graham Bell, who bankrolled the activities of an opposition organization, the American Association to Promote the Teaching of Speech to the Deaf.[6] It is against this backdrop of fear and alarm that these films were made.

The films of the Moving Picture Committee were sign language films, made silently as were other films of that time. No captions, other than the names of signers and the titles of their lectures, were added to the films. They were made to illustrate sign language in its "purest" form, to communicate across distance not by the written word, but by signs. For the first time, ideas could be transported to places around the country in the original language of Deaf people.

George Veditz, a prolific writer and orator, was nearing the end of his term as president of the NAD when he was selected to give a lecture on "The Preservation of the Sign Language" for one of the films. Also selected was Edward Miner Gallaudet, the president of Gallaudet College and the son of Thomas Hopkins Gallaudet, a founder of the first school for deaf children in Hartford, Connecticut. Because Gallaudet was seventy-five years old at the time he made his film, the committee knew this might be their only opportunity to record his signing. John B. Hotchkiss, stooped with age, was one of the few students still living who remembered Laurent Clerc, also a founder of the American School for the Deaf. His lecture, "Memories of Old Hartford," described an encounter with Clerc. Amos Draper, one of the first graduates of Gallaudet College, gave a lecture on the signing of the charter to authorize establishment of a college for deaf students. George Dougherty, a Deaf chemist, gave a brief lecture in front of a small audience on the invention of chloroform. Robert McGregor, the first president of the National Association of the Deaf, was filmed twice. First, he delivered a lay sermon, a sober exhortation to Deaf men and women to unite "as brothers and sisters under God." In his second appearance, "The Irishman and the Flea," he turned witty and ironic as he told of his search for a deaf person anywhere who suited the oralist ideal of someone who could speak without strain or effort. Invoking the racist story of an Irishman who could not catch an elusive flea on his body, McGregor said he rode trains and drove cars to try and track down deaf people who acted as if they were hearing, but no matter how far and wide he searched, such a person did not exist.

These films are precious. Written language can give clues to a language's history, but it changes far more slowly than speech. From descriptions of pronunciations of words, linguists can resurrect how spoken language sounded before voice recordings were invented. Likewise, sign linguists can study early sign language books from the nineteenth century with descriptions of signs to speculate how signs were made, but it is hard to capture a sense of the intonation, the flow, and the execution of a language from written records alone. The astonishing achievement of the NAD films is not only that they were made at all, or that they were made so early in the history of film, but also that there was such a range of signing preserved for the modern day, from older to younger signers, from hearing to Deaf, across many different topics. The window into the history of American Sign Language through these films is, fortunately for us, a wide one.

The NAD films have given linguists a treasure trove of examples of how signs have changed over time. Some signs are emblems of their era. The sign DOLLAR used by Veditz to explain how much money the committee wanted to raise involved a circular movement on his palm, to refer to the dollar coin. The modern sign for DOLLAR reflects the change to bills. In another example, McGregor uses a sign for TELEPHONE in which he holds two objects, one for the old speaker device and the other for the listening device.

Nancy Frishberg, one of the first linguists to study the films, found that a number of older signs were signed farther away from the body, at the sides, but over time, moved toward the center—for example, HELP in the older form was signed on the elbow, but now is signed on the hand. SORRY and LOVE were signed near the left side; today they are signed at the center of the body. Two-handed signs such as DEVIL are reduced to one-handed in modern forms. Historical change in signs involves moving them inward and simplifying them by reducing the number of hands to one.[7] Indeed, to look at the signing orators of this era is to watch them appear to sign very grandly, in part following oratorical tradition at the time, but also because both hands were used and many signs were at the outer periphery of the body.

To the modern signer, Veditz, E. M. Gallaudet, and their contemporaries on film, though still intelligible, are dated. For one thing, in the films, the signers demonstrate no mouth movement throughout the lecture. Today signers tend to move their mouths more visibly, in what are called "mouth gestures." In the films, the body was kept stiff and solidly anchored to the floor. Signers performing today allow the body to move more flexibly in the performance space. When Veditz fingerspelled, which he did liberally through his lecture, he made each letter of the word slowly and deliberately, moving his hand sideways as though marking positions on an invisible floating page. Fingerspelling in ASL today is much more rapid, each handshape quickly replacing the next, and the hand remains fixed in open space in front of the signer. There is a noticeable difference in the way the signs were articulated, in part because the signers were unsure of the capabilities of film, and wanted above all to be intelligible and clear for "future generations of signers." As the signers in 1913 looked into the lens of the camera, they tried to imagine audiences of the present and the future, in America and elsewhere in the world. No doubt, these were ambitious filmmakers.

Half a century after the films were made, they disappeared from popular use and were left in deep storage in the basement of the Gallaudet library. When sign language research began its ascent in the 1970s, the old films were remembered, retrieved, and shown again in restored form. Today they are widely available on video, and Veditz's famous lecture in particular is often shown in sign language and Deaf culture classes as an example of the old style of signing and the depth of feeling about sign language that existed at that time.[8] Nearly one hundred years later, images of George Veditz in tails and stiff collar, and Robert P. McGregor stretching his arms wide as he exhorted "brothers and sisters all over the land" to join together, still speak to Deaf people as powerfully as they did when they were first made.

Though the films were made nearly a hundred years after the first school for deaf children opened in 1817, many featured men and women who were young children or adults during the middle of the nineteenth century. John Hotchkiss was nearly eighty in his film, so his signing would still reflect what sign language probably looked like when he was a young adult, a tangible record of sign language form for modern-day linguists. Edward Miner Gallaudet, Amos Draper, and others were likewise filmed in their later years, preserving for the record, as the NAD wished, the sign language of their youth.

John Hotchkiss was a droll man, bouncing slightly at the knees, as he told of his encounter with Laurent Clerc while a pupil at the American School for the Deaf. Clerc, as Hotchkiss portrayed him, was by then an old man who used a cane, but he describes Clerc as full of warmth and good cheer. As he remembers him, Clerc was fond of aphorisms: first, that one should "*eat* to *live,* and *NOT, live* to *eat!*" Hotchkiss did a lively copy of Clerc himself, emphasizing in the first that one should "eat wisely" and in the second, not "gorge oneself." As he concluded his short segment, Hotchkiss pronounced that it would not be "long, long, *LONG!*" as he signed from the arch of his foot up through his leg and his arm to his shoulder, "before we meet again." The bit of humor, then as now, draws a smile because the sign LONG is normally signed only from the hand to the shoulder. Robert McGregor gave an accomplished sermon exhorting "all brothers and sisters to join as one nation under God." He is deeply serious in the film, a bit unsmiling, and perhaps over-rehearsed, but his generously large signing, as if from a distant pulpit, has endured as an example of early signed sermons.

After the films were made, the most frequently requested by audiences around the country was Edward Miner Gallaudet's "The Lorna Doone Country of Devonshire England." As the son of Thomas Hopkins Gallaudet, Edward was an embodiment of the earliest history of American deaf education. Compared to the other films, though, Gallaudet's is harder to follow. While the others are slower and careful, he almost rushes through his narrative. Instead of a personal narrative, Gallaudet chose to retell a popular fiction of his time, R. D. Blackmore's *Lorna Doone.* His signing is more abrupt and jagged, and the committee realized later that they had positioned him against an overly ornate backdrop, making his signing difficult to see.

Edward Miner Gallaudet's film was one of the first made by the committee, and they were disappointed in it. Veditz wrote to the chair of the Motion Picture Committee that the film "was made when the art of making these films was still crude."[9] The committee had previously approached Gallaudet and suggested that they make a second film but Gallaudet replied expressing much reluctance, saying that he thought the film was adequate, and furthermore, that at a recent exhibition those who had seen the film "expressed themselves as highly pleased and did not criticize it at all."[10] Still, Veditz would proclaim Gallaudet's film "the poorest in the lot."[11]

Of the NAD films, George Veditz's "The Preservation of the Sign Language" is by far the most impassioned and memorable. His lecture was original—not derived as many of the other films were from a popular poem or story, nor was it pedantic and cautious. Whereas other signers were rendered stiff by the presence of a camera, Veditz grew more confident and animated as he signed toward his powerful conclusion. Today, Veditz's film, not Gallaudet's, is the most frequently viewed. Its true effect lies in the blend of his powerful delivery and the evocativeness of his message. Like the film of Martin Luther King delivering his "I Have a Dream" speech, Veditz's film oratory has reached a kind of mystical plane. It is powerful enough to bring unexpected tears, and to call people to their feet cheering. For this accomplishment, captured on no longer than fourteen minutes of celluloid, George Veditz has become far more well-known than any of his contemporaries.

Politically moderate by nature, Gallaudet spoke out in support of sign language in education, but was not a fiery orator on the subject. Veditz, on the other hand, was an aggressive and impassioned advocate. His letters often had an acerbic edge to them when he wrote about his true feelings. In a letter to Roy Stewart, chair of the Moving Pictures Committee, Veditz wrote that he was quite unhappy with one of the recently completed films featuring superintendents of schools for the Deaf: "The galaxy of wooden Indians called by courtesy superintendents of our schools made me grunt. Why did not the critters use signs? ? ? ?" Veditz went on to insult each superintendent by name: "Why did not Harris Taylor instead of jabbering like a monkey at big-chin Bowles, sling a few signs that you an' me and the rest of the clan could understand? The only human being in the lot was Ray of North Carolina . . . Next time tell them that these films are to be SIGN LANGUAGE films and that they are expected to speak in our deafandum vernacular. If they kick, they can stay out."[12]

Veditz was a man of large ambitions and he carried out most of them. He lost his hearing from scarlet fever at the age of nine, and shortly after enrolled in Maryland School for the Deaf. Upon his graduation, he lacked funds to enter Gallaudet, so he worked for two years in the school's printing department, learning first-hand the trade he would later enter as writer and editor. He trained his deaf students for jobs in major newspapers and in printing houses around the area. After he entered Gallaudet he did so well that he graduated in 1884 with the highest record ever of any student at the college. He returned to Maryland School as a teacher and later moved to Colorado, where he became the editor of the *Silent Courier*, a Deaf newsletter. A restlessly curious man, he took up poultry farming, raised squabs, and dabbled with growing dahlias and gladiolas. Even while editor of his own newspaper, he regularly contributed pieces for other publications, including the *Silent Worker*, the official publication of the National Association of the Deaf, and the *Maryland Bulletin*, the Maryland School's newspaper. He also took on the editorships of *Western Poultry World* and the *Western Pigeon Journal*.[13] Upon his death, the *Maryland Bulletin* published short memorials from his students and colleagues. Many referred to his "vitrolic pen," and described him as a "relentless opponent."[14]

Today Gallaudet's stiff rendition of the story of Lorna Doone seems antiquated. As a retelling of a novel that has faded from popular memory, his lecture has little effect today other than the opportunity to see his sign language. Veditz, however, has managed to make his film timeless. In his crisp and forceful style, Veditz willed himself to speak out to Deaf people around the world and into future generations. And at that, he succeeded.

There have been several written translations of Veditz's signed lecture, including one by Carol Padden and another by Eric Malzkuhn, which were used to caption the film for modern use. Generally Veditz is not difficult to understand. Because the style at the time was to fingerspell not only single words but also entire phrases, particularly for oratorical emphasis, Veditz left precise clues for the English translations of some of the more emotional points in his speech. But in places, his sign phrasing is ambiguous, leading the translator to wonder whether Veditz intended one or two sentences, or a particular emphasis on one or another sign. Sign intonation in 1913 is significantly different from that used today, in part because of diachronic change in American Sign Language, and in part because of general style differences spanning nearly a century.

Through a wholly accidental and fortuitous discovery, a written version of Veditz's speech was recently found. Mike Olson, an archivist at Gallaudet University, was browsing through an antique shop in Maryland when he came across old postcards addressed to Roy Stewart. Recognizing the name, Olson contacted the dealer and discovered the dealer was a grandnephew of Stewart, and remarkably, had in his possession Stewart's entire collection of letters and records about the NAD film project. Included in the collection was a letter from George Veditz to Roy Stewart in which he complains about the superintendents' signing, and privately worries that in his own film, he looked like a "singed cat." Tucked inside his letter was his speech—typewritten by Veditz himself in English.[15]

The discovery of the lost records has opened up the NAD films to new interpretation. The deliberations of the film committee are brought to life again. Roy Stewart comes across as an able leader, shepherding the complicated project through to completion.[16] After years of soliciting contributions, the Moving Picture Committee succeeded in raising nearly $5,000. In later years, as more films made by other organizations were contributed to the committee, they worked to make those available for distribution as well. Stewart received numerous letters from Deaf leaders around the country, asking how to rent the films, and then later how to return them. After the first experiment in distribution, Stewart insisted that admission be charged for each showing, and that funds be used by the committee to make new prints from the negatives, to replace ones worn from repeated showings. Stewart also stipulated that groups desiring to rent the films had to hire an "experienced operator" who knew how to thread the film into the notoriously balky machines.[17] In one letter, the films were returned with complaints that the "tin boxes they are in are abominable. Sure you ought to get the right size, so they will fit in."[18] The letters represent a slice of film history just a decade after the medium was invented, showing how ordinary people interacted with the new technology.

The centerpiece of the recently recovered records is Veditz's written version of his own speech. We now can determine that for the most part, modern translations have followed much of Veditz's intent. As we place the English versions side by side, the modern translations and the Veditz original, even more evidence of language change in ASL is revealed. Recently Ted Supalla has been analyzing the old films for morphological change, or how signs change their internal word structure over time. He finds that many modern signs were historically phrases, where two or more signs were used; today a single sign remains. The modern sign SON was formerly a phrase, MALE ROCK-BABY, as signed by Edward Miner Gallaudet in his "Lorna Doone" narrative. Supalla argues that in diachronic change, phrases first become compounds, and later single signs in a process he calls "grammaticization." In this case, the two signs changed into a single sign, SON. In another example, the modern sign SUNDAY was formerly two signs, JESUS (or HANDS-RAISED) and DAY.[19]

In Veditz's speech, we see the older version of the modern sign WREATH, signed as GREEN WREATH. Today WREATH is signed alone without the color unless one wanted to make special note of the color, as in a "white wreath" or a "gold wreath." We also see that the superlative suffix in ASL, translated as " -est" in English, appeared first as a separate two-handed sign, MOST. Veditz uses two signs, POOR MOST, but translates it in his English version as a single word, "poorest." Modern ASL has a productive superlative suffix that can be added to many adjectives: for example, SMART-EST, "smartest," EASY-EST, "easiest." Furthermore, these examples are one-handed signs with suffixes, unlike Veditz's versions, which were two-handed as well as being two separate signs.

Stepping back, and viewing Veditz's English text as a whole, there is yet more to be seen. First, Veditz writes to Stewart that he is enclosing his copy of the speech, which he wrote *after* the film was made: "I have written down my address as well as I remember it . . . I think I got the main points in very near the order in which they were filmed."[20] Not surprisingly, the written version of the speech is slightly out of order with the actual speech in the film. His unforgettable biblical warning, "A new race of Pharaohs that knew not Joseph are now taking over the land and many of our American schools" appears near the end of his signed speech, but earlier in his written version. It is clearly better to use the powerful phrase at the end, as the speech builds to his final thundering proclamation: "We will all love and guard our beautiful sign language as the noblest gift God has given to Deaf people." Veditz also adds entire sentences to his written version that do not appear in the film, perhaps because he cannot resist improving on himself:

"These teachers are sacrificing them [deaf children] to the oral Moloch that destroys the mind and soul of the deaf." Later in his text he writes of his European friends, "These films are destined to cross the ocean and bring happiness to the deaf of foreign lands," but this sentence doesn't appear in the film either.

He takes further liberties with his written version. Some phrases in the original speech are given more elaborate versions in English. When he describes the envious eyes of the French and German Deaf people who see that Deaf Americans still have use of their sign language in some schools, he writes: "They look upon us as prisoners bound in chains look upon those who walk about free in God's open air." The last phrase, "in God's open air," is not said directly in the signed version. Later, Veditz describes oral teachers as refusing to listen to the pleas of Deaf people; instead they "cast them aside." In the written version, Veditz adds a flourish: "Their teachers have held them off with a hand of steel."

Written after the film was made, Veditz's "transcript from memory" may show that there was not an intent among Veditz and the committee to "translate" the films into English or to have an English interpretation of it accompany the film when it was distributed. In Veditz's time, there was more of a sense of separation between sign language and written English. To the early twentieth-century Deaf, the two languages were equally expressive, but it did not mean that they saw them as structurally equivalent. The idea to study signed speeches in detail and render close translations for them into speech or English is a recent development. Certainly the technology that exists today, which allows one to pause on a videotape or a DVD and study a single frame, permits the close comparison of ASL and English. But it would not have occurred to Veditz or his colleagues to try and match the two languages closely by phrase or sentence because they believed that not only did the languages differ, but their worlds of meaning were distinct, too.

From the collection of Roy Stewart's letters, it appears that the groups sponsoring the film exhibitions were almost always Deaf people: alumni associations, local Deaf clubs, Deaf churches. This does not mean that there were no hearing people in the audiences. In a letter to Roy Stewart, a Deaf man planning an exhibition of the films in his local community asks that Stewart send "papers" for the films so that they can be read aloud by a hearing person during the film, which suggests that the films were voiced into spoken English translation at least some of the time.[21] It is not clear who the voiced translations benefited exactly. Possibly hearing friends or relatives, but there is little mention of them in the letters. When Veditz rails in one film against "a new race of pharaohs who . . . do not understand signs for they cannot sign," it is hard to imagine a significant number of such "pharaohs" coming to see the films.

But at least one did just that. J. Schuyler Long gossiped in a letter to Roy Stewart that Frank Booth, the superintendent of the Nebraska School for the Deaf, showed up at a film exhibition in Omaha. A hearing son of Deaf parents, Booth became an ardent oralist and was widely despised by Deaf people for his rejection of sign language.[22] Long told Stewart: "You did not tell me that McGregor's flea story was on that film . . . And right there under Booth's nose those films were thrown on the screen and the oral method got it hard right in an oral hot bed . . . Of course I had to assure Booth that we were not trying to steal a march on him but since they were shown there without my knowledge in advance the joke was too good and we could not help but enjoy it."[23] Because he had Deaf parents, Booth knew sign language, and would have understood the films anyway.

As were all of the early films, these were silent films. Unlike silent films for hearing people, however, apparently no background music or sound effects were prepared to accompany them. Some silent films for the general public contained English text, but the only English text in any of the NAD films were the titles that introduced the subject of the film and the name of the signer, as in "The Preservation of the Sign Language, by George Wm. Veditz." There were no intertitles, or small signs representing dialogue inserted between film scenes, that later became popular in silent films. There were no subtitles; indeed subtitles as a way to represent language would not appear until much later, after talking films were developed. The signed speeches were presented in full body, from above the tops of signers' heads to below their feet. There were no close-ups, no changes in camera angle. All the speeches were signed without interruption, though it seems the films were spliced together in places, probably from breakage, causing brief "blips" in the film image.

Gallaudet gave his *Lorna Doone* narrative standing on the stage at Chapel Hall, one of the oldest buildings on the Gallaudet campus, and one with a great deal of symbolic meaning for alumni of the college. There can be no doubt that the films were meant for Deaf people, as Veditz says several times in his speech, as well as for their Deaf brothers and sisters elsewhere in the world who have "watched, with tear-filled eyes and broken hearts, this beautiful language of signs snatched away from their schools." What is notable about the intended audience for these films is that they were not speaking to hearing people who might, with a little knowledge and proselytizing, become converted to their cause, nor to those who were the objects of Veditz's fiercest condemnations. It was taken for granted that it would be difficult if not impossible to communicate to them through the language of signs, so their primary audience was each other, or those who knew the language.

The distance between Deaf people and their community of signers (which did include hearing signers like Edward Miner Gallaudet and Edward Allen Fay) on the one hand, and hearing nonsigners on the other, was deep and wide. Written language was often the medium of communication between the two groups, but not sign language. Self-expression to hearing people who did not already know sign language could not be imagined; instead the written language was used to communicate. Veditz railed against the school superintendents who failed to sign when in the presence of a Deaf audience, rendering their speech unintelligible. In effect, Deaf people felt themselves silenced by the difference between languages and by the fact that even hearing people who could sign would fail to acknowledge sign language at all, as did Edmund Booth and the school superintendents.

The problem of voice that Veditz and the committee struggled with was an old one. Deaf people knew from long experience that hearing people were unresponsive to Deaf people's expression of their "needs, wants, and desires," as Veditz pronounced. Indeed, using the reference to "pharaohs that knew not Joseph," Veditz despised hearing people who listened more carefully to others speaking on behalf of the Deaf but not to Deaf people themselves. To surmount the vast chasm that divided Deaf people and those who had control of their schools, the Moving Picture Committee mounted an offensive to collect oratory in their own language, but at first, this offensive could only be addressed to other Deaf people.

It was not by sign language but by written language that Deaf people believed they could communicate with hearing others. Veditz knew the power of the pen, and he wrote as often and as widely as he could. Olof Hanson, elected president of the NAD after Veditz finished his term, was also a prolific writer and an aggressive advocate of Deaf causes. Yet both understood the limitation of the written word in reaching out to Deaf people. The 1913 films were an opportunity to convey voice directly in the language of the community, and project it onto screens around the country, multiplying its effect many times over. Veditz and the Moving Picture Committee could imagine new audiences, broader and more far-reaching than they had known, who would see sign language in its "original purity." The language of signs had finally become the medium as well as the message. Now what remained was what to say and how to say it.

In his lecture, Veditz leans heavily on romantic and religious imagery. Teachers of the deaf refuse to listen to the "prayer of the deaf" in Europe, leading them to view with envious eyes Americans who still can sign as walking "about free in God's open air." And at the end of the film, Veditz raises his hands high above his head as he proclaims sign language as "the noblest gift God has given Deaf people." Having invoked an authority no less than God, Veditz brings his speech to a conclusion, bows reverentially, and leaves the stage.

Baynton describes the new generation of teachers of the deaf as unmoved by such sentiment; indeed, they dismissed such rhetoric as antiquated. They believed that the teaching of speech was needed in order to help the next generation of deaf children not only to communicate in spoken language, but also to leave behind the shackles of a primitive life, and the "clannishness" that results from Deaf people spending time together because they know only sign language.[24] Veditz's appeals to God only reinforced the view of sign language as a holdback to a time when emotion, not reason, prevailed. His speech most likely struck the "progressive" oralist educators as quaint and excessively emotional, even desperate.

For the most part, it appeared that the NAD films had no discernible effect. Oralism continued its relentless march through schools for the deaf. By 1920, the *American Annals of the Deaf* reported that 80 percent of all schools for the deaf listed the oral method as their primary method of instruction.[25] Baynton finds that except for some sign language speeches that were spoken into English by hearing colleagues as they were delivered at conventions of teachers of the deaf, Deaf people and their organizations, including the National Association of the Deaf, were largely excluded from these discussions. Hearing teachers who supported the manual approach were not effective advocates either: they often discouraged Deaf people from speaking before their colleagues, or did not invite them to places where they could speak on their own behalf. Deaf people were left to communicate their opposition almost entirely by writing.

If the films did not change the course of the oral movement at the beginning of the century, what did they accomplish? They introduced Deaf people to the possibility of self-expression, by visual means and through film. They made their language observable to themselves, available for critique, and critique it they did. Many letters to and from Roy Stewart and the Moving Picture Committee were about the content of the films, whether the signing was clear and how to improve the presentation. The voice of Deaf people, in its original form, brought about a new appreciation for the language. Very quickly Deaf people grew to appreciate the power of their own language on film. What remained was for them to persuade *others* of the communicative power of sign language and that Deaf people had something to communicate. This would take another half century to accomplish.

Signers today understand the Veditz speech not only because they recognize the signs, but also because they recognize the oratory. Veditz's speech is entirely familiar, even when transported in time nearly a hundred years. He is angry about the same things, and rails against the same people. He is passionate about the one thing that Deaf people cherish—their language. Not only his vocabulary and his sentence structure survive in modern ASL, but also his manner of making clear cultural themes and arguments.

The themes in George Veditz's "The Preservation of the Sign Language" continue to resonate in the twenty-first century. The alarm that Veditz sounded as he called for the use of film to preserve sign language for future generations still seems real today.

One could argue though that Veditz worried needlessly—after all, sign language survived another ninety years after his dire warnings, and today shows a surprising robustness. Interest in sign language exploded in the 1970s and 1980s, with many colleges and universities today offering classes in American Sign Language.[26] Indeed ASL is often the second most popularly enrolled language after Spanish on university campuses. Sign language has even been used in families that have no concern with deafness; some hearing parents are beginning to teach their infants basic sign vocabulary as a means of communicating with them before the onset of spoken language.[27] By any measure, sign language is not the oddity or the novelty it once was; it seems to have entered popular culture in a way that Veditz could hardly have imagined. Schools, too, appear to have turned back the oral tide. In a recent survey of schools and programs for deaf children, nearly all public or state-supported programs offer deaf children education in sign language.[28] Whereas oral curricula used to dominate state-supported and publicly funded schools, parents now can find sign language education for their children in a public school district or a special school.

Yet Veditz's warnings strike a chord in the Deaf community. When he rails about the "worthless, cruel-hearted demands of people that think they know all about educating the deaf but know nothing about their thoughts and souls, their feelings, desires, and needs," Deaf people cheer. Though Deaf people today are unlikely to recognize the religious reference to "a new race of pharaohs," when Veditz explains that "they do not understand signs for they cannot sign," Deaf people nod knowingly. When the film reaches its conclusion, Veditz signs a line many have memorized, that "we will all love and guard our beautiful sign language as the noblest gift God has given to Deaf people." It is remarkable, even astonishing, that Veditz could speak so directly and meaningfully to Deaf people today.

The film resonates because Deaf people still feel, deeply and with conviction, that their language is under threat. Genetic engineering has as its goal not the preservation of sign language, but the elimination of deafness so that no child will be consigned to using sign language. The popular media continue to write stories about children with cochlear implants who achieve the ability to hear and use speech, implying directly or indirectly that the child does not need sign language anymore because he or she has the possibility of speech.[29] Ironically, sign language is increasingly taught to hearing children in public schools at all levels as an option for foreign language instruction.[30] For ASL to be acceptable for hearing children, even beneficial to their early development as some have claimed, yet at the same time viewed as detrimental to the development of deaf children, is one of the oddest contradictions of our age.

Today as in 1913, Deaf people struggle with the problem of voice, how to make themselves heard over a powerful other voice of hearing people who define them and their needs differently. How can Deaf people explain why deafness and sign language should exist in an age of scientific advancement? How can they explain why sign language is necessary for young deaf children? Even today, sign language has a tinge of the romantic about it—the marvel of communicating not with voice but with the face, hands, and body—but that same romanticism can resign it to irrelevance. How can Deaf people make sign language relevant in the age of the genome and the microchip?

Sign language is relevant because it is a supreme human achievement, accomplished over a long history that has accumulated in time and in people, the collective genius of countless human beings. Deep in its structure are clues to the workings of the human brain and the wisdom of social groups that work together to make meaning and find a purpose for living. That Deaf people can preserve a sign language despite attempts to keep them apart from one another, and efforts to banish the use of the language from their schools, is testimony to why sign languages exist in the first place—as uniquely human inventions for the problem of how to transcend the individual and form social contact with others. Sign languages show what humans can do if they do not hear speech, and they show what signers can do *even* if they hear speech: they make and use language. We strive to make meaning in as many different ways and forms as we can. To express is divine.

In one of Veditz's last lines, he says: "as long as we have Deaf people on earth, we will have signs." It is an expression of hope and determination. Veditz fought against the prospect that there might be a time when there will be deaf people but no sign language. But his statement also implies that there may be a time when we will *not* have deaf people. Or that we will have a sign language but without Deaf people. Veditz's speech enlivens and guides Deaf people, for within his signs and in his written words, Veditz is very much the Deaf person his predecessors were, and very much the Deaf person we are today.

4
A New Class Consciousness

Ask any Deaf person over the age of seventy what they remember about the years during the Second World War, and they are likely to tell of the big Deaf clubs, the large halls where Deaf people met on weekend nights to play cards, watch beauty pageants, or socialize around a bar with one of the club officers as bartender. Deaf clubs were places where Deaf people could leave behind the drudgery of the factory and the anonymity of their neighborhoods and find respite with Deaf friends. Young children from those years will remember the picnics and the family events where children could play as their parents talked long into the night. Clubs sold beer and food and charged admission to cover the costs of the buildings they rented. Some made enough income from membership dues and food sales to buy their own building for a permanent clubhouse. Smaller, less affluent clubs rented floors, often in downtown buildings where rent was cheaper and trolley transportation was easy.

Today Deaf clubs are for the most part gone. There are a few remaining, but they are mostly populated by the elderly who still remember clubs as they once were. Indeed, these clubs are only a shadow of their past vitality. But through the 1960s, Deaf clubs were quintessential *places* in the community—many were owned by Deaf people. A typical club had a large hall where hundreds of people could meet, with side rooms for card playing. Often the halls featured a stage for lectures and entertainment. Some clubs had entire floors of buildings, with a room dedicated for the sports organizations and another for the officers of the club. A management structure took care of the details, from the club president down to the treasurer and the person who worked behind the bar selling drinks, later tabulating the profits for the clubhouse.

During the war years, Deaf people spent much of their leisure time at the local club: The larger ones were open daily and through the weekend, providing not only time with other Deaf people, but also entertainment of all types. The Hebrew Association of Manhattan regularly staged full-length theater productions, usually signed translations of popular plays, and so did other Deaf clubs.[1] Merv Garretson remembers that while he was working at the Montana School for the Deaf in 1951, the local Great Falls Club of the Deaf staged a full repertoire of plays, songs, and other performances. Between plays, clubs offered skits, beauty pageants, songs in sign, and in the 1960s, clubs could rent captioned films from a government-sponsored program, and using 16mm projectors, run their own small movie theaters in the clubhouse. In places like Chicago and New York City, clubs were virtual towns, with "mayors," "city councils," and "citizens" who voted on the actions of the club.

Most clubs participated in sports. The big clubs had basketball and softball teams and played against other clubs in regional and national tournaments. Home movies made in the heyday of Deaf clubs show tournament games followed by huge gatherings of Deaf people celebrating in large halls, lifting up drinks and cheering for the photographer. Trophies won were proudly displayed in glass cases in the clubhouse. In these home films we see shot after shot of packed halls and busy bartenders.[2] With so many people crowded together in one place, one can begin to imagine a nation of Deaf people, clustered in Deaf clubs across the country.

Ohio alone had at least one Deaf club in each of its major cities, Akron, Toledo, Cincinnati, Columbus, Cleveland, Warren, and Dayton. Nearly all of these major clubs owned their own building, and there were yet more in smaller cities, where the members rented instead of owned their space.[3] New York City had at least twelve different Deaf clubs, spread out across the boroughs. A destination for any Deaf person living in or visiting the city, the Union League was the largest and most popular of all; its doors were open daily and for long hours. Other clubs were mainly sports clubs: the Naismith Club in Brooklyn (named after James Naismith, the inventor of basketball), or the District of Columbia Club of the Deaf, where Carol Padden's father played basketball for a few years after he graduated from Gallaudet in 1945. Some clubs in New York City were oral-only, like the Laro Club ("oral" spelled backwards) and the Merry-Go-Rounders, where signing was prohibited. There were ethnic clubs as well, including the Hebrew Association of the Deaf in Manhattan and another Hebrew association in Brooklyn.[4]

Deaf clubs divided along ethnic and racial lines. In large urban areas, there were Jewish or Hebrew Deaf clubs that in the early part of the twentieth century helped to socialize deaf immigrants to American life. Like deaf schools, Deaf clubs were segregated places. The National Association of the Deaf refused membership to African-American Deaf citizens, citing bylaws of their organization that limited membership to "any white deaf citizen."[5] The Union League prided itself on its popularity and prominence in New York City but its constituency specifically excluded African-American Deaf members. Alongside white clubs, there were Black Deaf clubs; one of the oldest was the Washington Silent Society, which later became the Capital City Association of the Deaf, located not far from the white club, the District of Columbia Club of the Deaf. In Los Angeles, there was the Blue Jay Club, and in Atlanta, the Ebony Club. Cleveland had two clubs; the Black club was the Cleveland Silent Athletic Club and the white, the Cleveland Association of the Deaf. The Imperials Club in New York City didn't have a fixed location; instead meetings were held in a member's home in Harlem.[6]

The segregation mirrored a deep division among African-American and white Deaf workers through the war years. Two large employers during the Second World War and in the years shortly after, Goodyear Aircraft and Firestone Tire and Rubber Company of Ohio, aggressively recruited women and Deaf people, but did not hire many African-American workers, either Deaf or hearing.[7] The largest employer for African-American Deaf workers in Ohio was not in Akron, where many white Deaf people found work in the tire industry, but in Cincinnati at a bible publishing company, the World Publishing Company. These workers would later open the Cincinnati Charter Club for Black Deaf members in the city.[8]

Though prohibiting African-American athletes from joining as members, white Deaf clubs aggressively pursued them to play for the club teams. Top basketball players of the time like Glenn Anderson, Leon Grant, and Tom Samuels were eagerly sought after by coaches because any one of them could take a team to the national championships. Coaches would offer money and jobs, as players moved from one powerhouse club to another in search of the best offer. But these star players could not enter the clubroom, or join as members. Glenn Anderson had just moved to Detroit in the fall of 1970 when a member of the Motor City Association of the Deaf approached him and asked if he would play on their team. Anderson remembers he was at the club's bowling night with friends watching white members play when he told the club leader he would consider playing basketball only if the club would first allow African-American men and women to bowl as well. The leader refused, and in retaliation, organized a campaign to dismiss Anderson from his position as a jobs counselor in Detroit.

Clubs also drew in Deaf people from oral schools who wanted to make contact with other Deaf people. Even though there were oral-only clubs, many became socially involved in the signing community through the larger clubs. Clubs served as socializing institutions, places where one could go to learn to be Deaf, to enjoy the company of other Deaf people and the ease of communicating, perhaps for the first time in one's life. Many people brought up in an oral-only environment, referred to as "ex-oralists" by Deaf people, found the clubs to be immensely appealing for the opportunity they provided to meet others like themselves.

Clubs were also places where Deaf people could find leads for a job. Club memberships were often made up of people who worked in the same place or in the same line of work. The Union League in New York City was heavily populated by Deaf printers, as was the Chicago Club of the Deaf. Both were well-known for their weekend-night poker games, which attracted Deaf men with enough income to spend on card games. Functioning like "hiring halls," these clubs were the main contact point for newcomers to a community as well as for members in search of new jobs. They were also an outlet and a resource for people experiencing problems in the workplace.

Bernard Bragg and Eugene Bergman's play *Tales from a Clubroom* was written in the waning days of Deaf clubs when they were fast becoming more nostalgic than essential.[9] Set in a typical Deaf club, Bragg and Bergman populate the play with archetypal characters, from the busybody wife of the club president to the embezzling treasurer who is exposed by club members. In this scene from the play, we see a typical discussion about work:

Grady: . . . I heard that you lost your job. Is it true?
Futrell: Boy, news sure travels fast in the deaf world, Yes, I was laid off last week, after 15 years. So I started looking for a new job. I went to a place that advertised for skilled car mechanics. There were five other applicants, all hearing except me. They were snotnoses, fresh from school. I filled out the application

form, but they hired one of those green kids. They said the job required a lot of talking, and a deaf man couldn't handle it. Bullshit! I told them no engine ever talked to anybody, and that I understood cars better than most hearing mechanics . . . They gave me the brushoff. They didn't want to be bothered.

Yakubski: I know how you feel.

Mrs. Futrell: (To Yakubski.) Please help my husband. Can you do something?

Yakubski: Well, I'm not a lawyer, but I understand there are new government laws, like Section 504 that say deaf people have equal rights. I'll give you the business card of a man to see. If anyone can help, he can.

One could get other kinds of information as well. Before more sophisticated technology became available for doorbells and phones, clubs served as a place to find someone who could rig up flashing lights to alert Deaf people that someone was at the door, that the phone was ringing, or that the baby was crying during the night. A common system was a Sears garage-door opener transmitter and receiver, which, with a soldering iron and some wire, could be rigged into a light flashing system activated by a doorbell, a phone circuit, or a microphone. A character from the play, Grady, was the local expert in the technology:

Futrell: Hi! Hey, look at those wires for the flasher. They're a fire hazard! This place would never pass a fire inspection.

Yakubski: So—go ahead and fix it.

Futrell: Let me see . . . very strange. Who installed it?

Yakubski: Grady.

Futrell: It shouldn't work at all. What a mess!

Yakubski: Been working fine for four years now.

Tales from a Clubroom picked up on typical tensions in clubs, among workers, and between oral and signing Deaf people. In their heyday, Deaf clubs were populated by Deaf workers of all types, from printers and carpenters, to shoemakers and tailors, to some who were not working, at least not "legitimately." These were the Deaf peddlers who sold trinkets and alphabet cards on the streets, in the trolleys and at the train station, wherever there were crowds of people. At the Chicago Club of the Deaf, peddlers mingled alongside Deaf printers, causing tension and resentment over who was legitimately working. At one time, the president of the Chicago Club tried to deny entrance to peddlers, posting signs inside the club saying they would not be welcome because they denigrated others who did not "beg" for pity and for small payments from hearing people.[10] In this fictional Deaf club, Collins is a judgmental young outsider, an "ex-oralist," whom Carswell, a local peddler, calls a "damn hippopotamus" because of his exaggerated mouth movements:

Collins: (To Carswell.) Someone told me that you sell ABC cards. Is that true?
(Yakubski gestures "Quiet" behind Carswell's back to Collins.)
Carswell: So what! Is that any of your business?
Collins: Our business! Yes! All of us here are deaf, too. You got nerve to come here when you are spoiling the name of us deaf by begging.
Carswell: Damn hippopotamus! I don't like the way you talk. *(They scuffle a bit before being separated, and Yabuski takes Collins aside.)*
Yakubski: What's gotten into you? I'm surprised at you.
Collins: How dare that beggar, that repulsive creature come here and mix with us!
Yakubski: (Mouths words at Collins.) What gives you the right to speak for all deaf people? You think he isn't one of us? How do you know? What makes you so sure?
Collins: But how do you all accept a man who spoils the name of the deaf? He makes hearing people despise deaf people.

Greene: (Puts cigar on edge of table, mouths words at Collins.) We accept
   him. You can see for yourself; he is here. We didn't kick him
   out! But we could kick you out for causing a disturbance!
Yakubski: The hearies already think so little of the deafies, what's
   the difference? What's more, we think a lot of Carswell. He's a
   big man here. He makes more money than all the other people
   here. We respect him because he fools the hearies. They always
   take advantage of the deaf, but that peddler, a deafie, takes advantage of them for a change. Can't you see that?

In this fictional club, the members give Collins a choice to apolo-
gize to Carswell for insulting him or be tossed out of the clubroom.
Collins, realizing the prospect of life without entry to the club,
goes to Carswell and apologizes and they end up drinking a toast
to "Deaf Power!" In the end, the Deaf club members, forced to
choose between a signing peddler and an ex-oralist, sided with the
peddler. Signing trumps begging. Carswell is one of them in a way
that Collins is not.

Despite a fondness for clubs so obviously projected in *Tales from a
Clubroom,* such clubs had already begun their deep decline by the
time the play was written. The venerable Union League, founded
in 1886 by graduates of the Institution for Improved Instruction of
Deaf-Mutes in New York City, grew to become one of the largest
Deaf clubs in the country. In an ad appearing in the July 1953 issue
of the *Silent Worker,* a magazine of the National Association of the
Deaf, the Union League touted its hours as "open daily from noon
to midnight." Thirty-three years later, the club had barely enough
members for a meeting, and decided the end was near. Going out
with a bang, the members threw themselves a large banquet, celebrating the end of a long and illustrious history.

Black Deaf clubs are mostly gone now too, replaced, in part, by a national organization, the Black Deaf Advocates, which has chapters in the same cities where clubs used to exist. Many of the clubs' former activities such as entertainment and socializing have transferred to the new organization, but the goal is oriented more to advocacy. Deaf clubs responded to a social structure that is changed today; instead of oralists and manualists, Black and white, athletes and nonathletes, there are now different ways of organizing and new kinds of affiliations. Sports clubs have shrunk in prominence and some have been replaced by national recreational associations, organized for a broader range of leisure and recreational activities such as camping and off-road bicycling.

Where local clubs once housed Deaf workers of different kinds, from carpenters and shoe repairers to teachers of the deaf, now there are professional associations for psychologists, sign language teachers, rehabilitation counselors, academics, and teachers of the deaf. Instead of clubs vying for members, there is a new landscape of Deaf social service agencies that provide job training and advocate for civil rights, including the right to interpreters and other social services. Membership no longer defines Deaf people's associations; instead participation is based on need. Whereas clubs once were divided by work lives, race, and sports, Deaf organizations today exist along dimensions of civil rights, citizenship, and professions, which are very much of the twenty-first century.

Technology is often blamed for the demise of Deaf clubs. Sometimes when Deaf people talk about the disappearance of the clubs, they point to the timing of certain technologies. For example, unlike the 1950s when Deaf people could not use the telephone or understand the spoken dialogue of popular films and television, Deaf people today have a wide array of telecommunication devices available to them. With a teletype device, Deaf people can use the telephone to send text messages, and with the decoder chip, they can watch captioned television and home videos. As the explanation goes, once they began using the new technologies, they lost interest in the Deaf clubs and stopped going. Since Deaf people could reach each other by phone, they no longer needed to visit the clubs to make arrangements to meet friends and stay in touch. Club skits and beauty pageants seemed like amateur pursuits compared to the entertainment value of the home television. Deaf people abandoned the club because technology freed them from having to visit it. This account of why the Deaf clubs disappeared has a ring of truth to it: It pays homage to technology and credits it with the power to alter lifestyles and social behaviors.

But the explanation cannot be entirely correct. The Deaf club was already on the wane by the time most of this modern technology became available. Teletypewriter machines for the telephone were growing in popularity among Deaf people through the 1960s, but they were still a novelty, and out of reach in price and accessibility to the working-class Deaf people who made up most of the membership of Deaf clubs.[11] Telephone access exploded in the 1980s, *after* clubs had started to see their membership numbers decline.[12] The first decoder device allowing captions to appear on television became available for purchase in 1978, a good ten years after many clubs had already closed. Though many clubs remained open through the end of the 1980s, their memberships had declined dramatically.

A more likely account is that Deaf clubs declined because of powerful shifts in Deaf people's work lives leading to the growth of a Deaf middle class. The kinds of work Deaf people did changed between 1940 and 1980, and the shift affected the kinds of spaces they used and the ways they interacted with one another. To understand this one has to understand how Deaf clubs came into being and who populated them.

Deaf clubs were built by Deaf people employed in factory and industrial kinds of occupations. Robert Buchanan describes this era as marking the transition of Deaf men and women from artisan jobs such as shoe repair and tailoring at the start of the century to more machine-based work in the years leading up to the First World War.[13] As war was declared in the spring of 1917, American industrial capacity quickly expanded, creating an immediate need for labor. With hearing men off to war, the industries turned to recruiting workers from other populations, including women and Deaf people.[14] Factories in Akron, Ohio, posted recruitment signs exhorting Deaf workers to apply, and Deaf workers eagerly passed them on to friends in Deaf clubs around the country. By the Second World War, industrial jobs became more commonplace for Deaf workers, leading many to abandon less well-paying jobs in the "solitary trades," such as baking, woodworking, upholstering, and shoe repair.

Home films of Deaf clubs showed them heavily populated by the quickly expanding class of Deaf workers. The Akron Club for the Deaf was so popular in the war years that it remained open seven days a week, twenty-four hours a day to accommodate Deaf workers at Goodyear Aircraft Company (GAC).[15] The GAC was a huge industrial complex, built in very short order to assemble fighter planes, blimps, and other forms of transportation needed to support America's entry into the Second World War. In 1941, Goodyear Aircraft sent out a nationwide call for workers, and it hired every man and woman it could, including Deaf people. Literacy levels were not tested, and if the person appeared reasonably able-bodied, he or she was hired, despite having no experience in the building of aircraft, or in manufacturing operations. The GAC was a classic Second World War industry, designed to accommodate large groups of untrained workers toiling long hours at specific tasks, managed by a few highly skilled managers.[16]

John Bradley, a resident of Kent, Ohio, remembers that his Deaf parents had learned at the Deaf club in New Jersey that Goodyear was hiring Deaf people in Akron, so they moved the family there. His father immediately got a job as a riveter though he had no previous experience. His mother assembled small parts in another part of the factory. He remembers barely literate Deaf people being hired at the GAC, but it didn't matter because there were so many jobs to be filled, including lower-level jobs packing boxes and moving goods from one part of the plant to another. Buchanan estimates that as many as a thousand Deaf workers were employed within the Goodyear company alone.[17] Deaf people would get off one shift, leave the plant, and meet Deaf friends coming in to begin the next shift. Instead of meeting between shifts to catch up with friends, Deaf leaders in Akron opened a club, and in short time, the Akron Club for the Deaf became a place to go to unwind from the long hours of work. There was such a large influx of Deaf people in the city, a virtual population boom, that the club became the best place to meet friends and, for many young single Deaf men and women, a way to scout out possible marriage partners.

The pattern was repeated throughout the country, spurred in part by the quick expansion of factory jobs during the war years. Barbara Kannapell has tracked Deaf people ranging from small groups of ten or twenty to hundreds and thousands working for the war effort in cities throughout the country, from Los Angeles and San Francisco to Dallas, St. Louis, and Baltimore. As communities of workers grew, Deaf clubs grew to dot the landscape as well, to fill the need for social time at the end of a long day.

Roger Scott trained as a printer during the war years, and after short stints at a small local newspaper, and then at the *Washington Star*, an afternoon paper in Washington, D.C., Scott moved to the Government Printing Office (GPO). The GPO was hiring deaf printers to meet an increased demand for production of government documents. As the federal office responsible for distributing official documents, including the *Congressional Record*, the GPO also published free materials on matters of public information, from how to use government services to information for farmers on how to build barns and water ponds. Scott rose through the ranks to become a floor supervisor, and retired in 1990 after thirty years at the GPO. By the time he retired, he had made the transition from the bulky machines and lead type of Linotype—which was the dominant technology in printing for more than a hundred years—to computers. When he began working at the GPO in 1959, there were nearly nine thousand workers, 150 of them Deaf. After the transformation in the printing trade, the GPO now employs less than a third of its former workforce, two thousand workers, of which only ten are Deaf.[18]

By the time Scott joined the GPO, he was part of a large population of Deaf printers, nearly all members of the powerful International Typographical Union (ITU), which strictly controlled access to the shop floor. The union required a six-year apprenticeship during which men and women worked with skilled printers on the floor. After this training, if they qualified, they could receive an ITU card that permitted them to work in any union shop in the country as either a permanent worker or a substitute ("sub").[19] Nearly every major newspaper, from the *Washington Post* to the *Chicago Tribune*, as well as the GPO, were union controlled, and thus available to Deaf workers with ITU cards. The union was so successful that it raised the wages and benefits of its workers to a level high enough that printing paid better than nearly any other trade that Deaf people could enter. For many Deaf men looking for a living wage that could support a family, printing was their best choice, and indeed, many entered the trade. The union allowed Deaf members to gain access to work where under other circumstances, they might be denied a job because of deafness. Moving through the ranks was fairly straightforward, because Deaf men could expect regular wage increases, bargained on their behalf by the union leaders. And finally, in places like the GPO and the *Washington Post*, there were good numbers of Deaf coworkers, making the workplace less solitary.

After the Second World War, as the country shifted to peacetime industries, the factories that once employed Deaf people in large numbers began to shut down, forcing Deaf men to search elsewhere for jobs. Many Deaf men returned to printing. A Deaf man who knew Roger Scott's family enrolled Scott as an apprentice in the printing program at the local Boys and Girls Club in Washington, D.C. The six years of apprenticeship included learning to use the special keyboard of Linotype machines and to operate the machine.

Linotype machines used a different keyboard than a typewriter, with lowercase letters grouped on the left, and uppercase on the right side. In the middle were all other characters, including punctuation and special symbols. Unlike on a typewriter, the spacebar was a long band on the left side. A Linotypist worked line by line; after composing the words for a single line, the "matrix" or mold would be directed to another part of the machine where spaces would be inserted between words in order to form a line. Following this, lead would pour into the matrices to form "slugs," or the lead type to be arranged for printing galleys. A skilled Linotypist made sure there were the minimum number of words and spacers in each line so that when hot lead flowed into the mold, there were no gaps through which lead could leak or spray. A Linotype operator knew not only how to type, but also how to keep the machine working through the many steps and importantly, how to avoid injury from hot lead.

After the requisite six years, Scott applied for union membership with the help of an older Deaf man at the local club. For Deaf men like Scott, working in the 1950s and 1960s meant working without much of what Deaf people use routinely today. Whereas today Deaf people can use interpreters to coordinate work with hearing coworkers and can compel employers to provide means of access to the workplace, Scott and his Deaf coworkers had no such benefit, requiring them to use other means to gain advantage on the shop floor. Meetings of union workers on a shop floor, called "chapel meetings," were as frequent as once a month, but none were ever interpreted for the Deaf union members. Scott remembers relying on a hard-of-hearing coworker to explain the discussions during a meeting, or on a hearing coworker who could fingerspell a few words.

Access was tentative, irregular, and incomplete, yet Deaf workers needed to know how to get enough information to understand their rights as workers, both within the union and in the company. There were complex rules and regulations within the union about the division of labor on the shop floor, including which worker was qualified for which type of work, how to acquire seniority and other benefits, and how to work with company bosses.[20] Before elections, typically for the shop steward who would serve as the union's representative on the floor and for the different officers of the chapel, Scott remembers that the Deaf workers exchanged information to avoid being taken advantage of. A hearing coworker would point at a name on a ballot and wink, but the Deaf workers would meet among themselves to decide which candidate would best represent them on the floor.

ITU cards were valuable, since they not only allowed access to union shops, but also permitted Deaf men and women to travel to other cities and work as substitutes in other shops. Unmarried Deaf men with wanderlust in their hearts and a yearning for adventure would travel from city to city, often following Deaf club basketball games. They could almost always count on a regular to call in sick or go on vacation and they could be hired as "subs," working often for as long as they wanted to stay. A skilled Linotypist could count on working almost every day, because floor shift managers always needed workers who could copy from written pages exactly as read, with few errors. Since all union shops had the same machinery and fixed divisions of labor, moving between different shops was fairly easy.

Like typewriters in the age of computers, Linotype machines have become obsolete, replaced by newer technologies with different modes of training. The computer does not require such a long apprenticeship, nor as many workers. The apprenticeship of printing that bound together Deaf printers within a shop and across shops has all but disappeared. Other types of trades for Deaf men, including shoe repair, upholstery, and bakery work, have also changed: Shoes are more likely to be discarded than repaired; likewise, sofas and chairs. Bakeries have become larger and more mechanized, changing the place of workers. Replacing older forms of work is a different pattern of work life, with sharp divisions between kinds of work that Deaf people do, where they work, and what training they undergo. This shift in work deeply influenced Deaf social institutions, notably the Deaf club.

Deaf clubs began their decline in the late 1960s. Attendance fell off precipitously, and membership rolls shrank. With diminishing funds, many were forced to sell off buildings. Some clubs, particularly in major cities, tried to revive interest by moving their rented spaces from less attractive urban areas to more suburban locations, but with little effect. Even as Deaf people bemoaned the decline, and tried with all good intentions to encourage friends to return, they themselves had already stopped going to club events. Clubs reduced their hours from daily to weekends only, then to once a month. Through the 1980s, the Metropolitan Washington Association for the Deaf offered special events a few times a year, but without a club structure or a building, the events were difficult to organize. Today, the very few Deaf clubs that remain are in places like Akron and Kansas City, where the elderly come for the memories of years past and the experience of being together with friends as they have done for nearly all their lives.

The transition was remarkably short. In little more than a decade, old types of work ceased, and new kinds of occupations opened up. A key influence was the increasing availability of professional occupations for Deaf men and women. As the public sector underwent a massive expansion in the early 1960s, jobs opened up in government-sponsored rehabilitation programs and in educational administration. In 1961, as Jack Gannon describes it, "six printers, five Linotype operators, nine teachers . . . an aircraft sheetmetal mechanic, a carpenter, an architect, a tax attorney and a rubber worker" were invited to a workshop to discuss how to involve Deaf people in professions that provided training and education to deaf children and adults.[21] Called the Fort Monroe Workshop, the organizers sought out Deaf leaders from clubs and shop floors as prospective employees for the public sector. Carmen Ludivico had been working as a Linotype operator at the *Pittsburgh Star* when he was invited to attend the Fort Monroe Workshop. He had developed a reputation among his coworkers as a level-headed leader on the shop floor, but he had never before been in the company of government workers, nor had he ever attended a professional "workshop." For him and others who came to the workshop, the event opened up the possibility of different kinds of careers, of training for different kinds of jobs.[22]

Deaf education as a field underwent change as well. In addition to printing, teaching in schools for the deaf was another stable job for Deaf men and women. Graduates of Gallaudet College through the 1960s could find employment at one of the many schools for the deaf throughout the country. Merv Garretson, a graduate of Gallaudet in 1947, moved to Great Falls, Montana, and worked as a printer while also teaching at the school. But by the late 1960s, education underwent massive reform, requiring that its teachers train for credentials and study for advanced degrees in order to receive employment.

As Deaf men and women pursued professions in education and the public sector, it became more obvious that there was a class divide between those who pursued professional careers and those who still worked in the trades, including in printing, and increasingly, in manufacturing jobs. Deaf clubs began to experience new tensions as distinctions between members and their occupations became more obvious. Deaf people in professions saw the clubs as an anachronism, a holdover from a time when Deaf people could only do certain kinds of jobs and were isolated from the mainstream. The characteristically urban environments that many Deaf clubs occupied only further emphasized the divide—as Deaf people moved to the suburbs, they identified with middle-class life, leaving behind the older and more urban life that Deaf clubs represented. Instead of building new clubs in the suburbs, the Deaf middle class turned more to professional affiliations, identifying themselves increasingly by job and profession such as education or rehabilitation.

Not only were clubs meeting places, but many of them were also permanent brick-and-mortar buildings, located materially in the lives of Deaf people. These buildings have nearly all been sold off. In their place is a more fluid community, where meeting spaces are borrowed and temporary. Deaf professionals attend conferences and workshops in borrowed hotel ballrooms and meeting spaces, gathering for a few days and then leaving until the next meeting is scheduled. As Deaf people moved into new kinds of work that brought them into new workspaces interacting with hearing people, their image of themselves that they wanted to project into public space changed. Their past as an almost exclusively working-class community became a mixed memory; instead, as Deaf people asserted their middle-class ideals and middle-class ambitions, they drifted away from the clubs. Playing poker at the local Deaf club or hosting skits seemed out-of-date. As cultural institutions and physical spaces, clubs became identified with an older way of life that held little attraction for the newly emerging professional class.

Even if one wanted to resurrect Deaf clubs, it would be hard to do so, and one could argue that much of the nostalgia about Deaf clubs is misplaced. Middle-class Deaf people may regret their passing, but most have no real interest in maintaining them. Once powerful political centers, they also practiced racism and sexism, perpetuating in the clubs what was already going on in the Deaf schools. Tensions among workers of different types, once tolerated in the fictional *Tales from a Clubroom*, now seem embarrassing.

It may be that Deaf clubs disappeared because their activities have been recreated in other forms by other organizations. Instead of being limited to amateur productions of the Hebrew Association of the Deaf in Manhattan, Deaf people can opt to watch a popular musical on Broadway with sign language interpreters, or to watch television and captioned video at home. With interpreting and access laws, the number of opportunities for culture and social interaction have expanded many times over. Much of the former function of Deaf clubs—to support a network for information about jobs and social life—has shifted to social service agencies that provide job training, peer counseling, and workshops on medical and social topics ranging from AIDS to disability rights. Whereas Deaf clubs were primarily social places to go after work, newer social service agencies are more business oriented, with larger organizations running profitable businesses on the side. A few have bought their own buildings: Greater Los Angeles Association of the Deaf (GLAD) and Community Services for the Deaf of South Dakota (CSD) are among the most successful, using funds from foundations and burgeoning nonprofit business ventures. Deaf clubs had poker games on weekend nights, but such gatherings do not occur at the new agencies. The social space of clubs has been replaced by commercial spaces—instead of a card game room, there are bookstores where sign language books and flashing light alarm clocks can be purchased. Instead of a large hall where members could celebrate a tournament championship, agencies have rooms for counseling, training, and other services. Whereas Deaf people could hang out for hours in the large club hall, today they may visit the agency if they have an appointment to see a counselor, or to conduct business while there. The agencies no longer provide free and unstructured social time.

The pattern is replicated across the country. In San Diego, Deaf and hearing people gather at a beachtown coffeehouse on Fridays. Deaf Women United, a national organization of Deaf women, meets every two years for four days in a hotel. On a borrowed or rented stage, there are performances and speeches along with workshops and discussion groups organized in hotel meeting rooms. There are no more informal, drop-in social spaces like clubrooms. William Leach asks whether the quality of these ephemeral interactions in borrowed and temporary spaces is the same as those carried out when social obligations to one another are linked to more permanent social spaces. Indeed people now have more options to participate in mainstream spaces, but what will replace the older sense of belonging to a community and having responsibilities to one's fellow citizens?[23]

In writing about the disappearance of place in American life, Leach laments that the temporariness of modern existence will eventually be fatal to American culture. As material spaces for meeting disappear in favor of more metaphorical or "virtual" spaces such as chatrooms or temporary hotel rooms, people themselves will in time dissolve their obligations to one another. When movements become ephemeral, easy, and without responsibility, individuals can even forget why they should have any such obligations. As town centers empty in favor of shopping malls, Leach wonders if individuals will become unrooted and America will essentially become "a country of exiles," made up of people who in time will become strangers to one another.

Together with the redesign and closure of some deaf schools, the disappearance of most Deaf clubs signifies a transitional moment in the social history of the community. Instead of materially segregated spaces where the boundaries are clearly marked—a wrought-iron fence around a deaf school or three-story buildings owned by Deaf clubs—the spaces have become fluid and symbolic. Deaf people today talk more about culture, community, and language, using a changed vocabulary to stake out boundaries. When older spaces existed, the idea and the phrase "Deaf culture" had yet to develop. At the height of Deaf clubs' popularity, there was no "American Sign Language"; indeed, the National Association of the Deaf's *Silent Worker* pronounced in 1950 that the sign language had "no grammar."[24] Today, with a sophisticated vocabulary for the language, culture, and practices of the community, boundaries are noted, marked, and debated, often just as heatedly as arguments had erupted between members in *Tales of a Clubroom* about whether a peddler belonged in a Deaf club. But can words replace brick-and-mortar places?

There are still a few *places* left in the community: notably schools for the deaf, and Gallaudet University, the oldest university for deaf people in the world. In many of these places, the original buildings have become historical landmarks, marking a time when Deaf people expected to live in separate spaces, apart and aside. Many schools for the deaf have libraries and museums to store the paraphernalia of the past: photographs of schools at a time when they were populous but segregated; trophies of sports played against schools that have since closed; and folders upon folders of old school materials.

To visit these spaces now, even in their redesigned form, is still to be aware of how unusual they are, compared to the modern context. Deaf people visit them more as tourists than occupants, aware that within their walls is a memory of not only a different time, but also a different kind of life. Indeed, the geography of the Deaf community has shifted; no longer is there a direct path from the schools to the clubs and the workplaces. Today, the community has arrivals from many places, from mainstream programs for deaf children in public schools as well as deaf schools. It would be wrong to describe the changed community as excessively fragile or tenuous. Deaf communities have always relied on borrowed spaces, or buildings controlled by others, even as Deaf people owned some of their own buildings. While spaces have changed, the strong rhetoric of self-preservation and independence has not.

5

Technology of Voice

It is easy to think of the human voice as inaccessible to deaf people. They do not hear their own voice nor do they hear the voice of others, so it must not be known to them. Indeed, for much of Deaf people's history, their name for themselves has been "deaf-mutes." In the 1913 films made by the National Association of the Deaf, the sign DEAF was two signs, the index finger contacting the ear and then contacting the mouth. It has since simplified into a single sign, but the history of the older sign is preserved in the two parts of the modern sign, where the finger still contacts at the ear and the mouth. Not long before the films were made, however, the term "mute" had begun to fall out of favor. In 1889, the *American Annals of the Deaf and Dumb*, a journal of deaf education, proposed that the title of the journal change, leaving only the simpler term, "deaf."[1]

The editors believed the term was misleading; deaf people were not entirely mute. Some were hard-of-hearing and could speak reasonably well; yet others had speech training and could use the voice. Deaf people disliked "mute" for a different reason—over the years, the word had come to mean an inability to speak on one's behalf, a lack of voice. Further, mute and dumb were increasingly being used in the popular literature to mean "lack of intelligence" more often than lack of ability to speak (as in "to be struck dumb"), leading Deaf people to advocate abandoning the descriptors.[2]

In fact, the human voice is an object, a property that Deaf people care about greatly, and through their history, it has been an object for them to "manage." They have often borrowed the voice of a relative or a friend, and more recently of an employee, to use for communicating with others. It is in this sense that voice can usefully be thought of as a technology: it is not merely a biological quality or a medium of expression, but an entity to be cultivated, managed, and most recently, converted into a commercial commodity. The management of the human voice today has become a multimillion-dollar industry, as Deaf people employ interpreters to translate for them into voice, and telephone companies hire voice operators to communicate for Deaf people over the telephone. The rapid expansion of voice into wireless and web technology has opened up even more ways to manage, shape, redirect, and indeed, profit from human voice for people who do not use it or hear it. As Deaf people have moved from separate lives within their communities, to lives in front of others, their management of voice has changed as well. They use voice to say different things now, to explain themselves and to participate in different ways. The properties of human voice have likewise changed, to become less intimate over the years, as Deaf people "contract" with an interpreter or an operator to voice on their behalf.

For most of its history, Deaf theater or "sign language theater" did not require voice; indeed, it was intended for a signing audience. Today almost all theater with Deaf actors will be accompanied by voice. The history is in part about changing audiences, from within the community to more public arenas. The transition in how voice came to be used in theater, first to "read" the lines, then to "interpret," and now, as "dual performance," where sign language and spoken language are presented simultaneously on the same stage, mirrors the transition from private to public forms of expression. But the change was not without consequence; as Deaf actors blended voice with sign language performance, their style of performing changed. Finding themselves no longer on stage alone, but working with speaking actors, Deaf actors changed how they performed, and they changed their choice of material to perform.

The few films of the Los Angeles Club for the Deaf during the 1940s that have survived featured the style of performance favored at the time: vaudeville shows, short comedy skits, and even dreadful blackface performances, alternating with beauty pageants and awards ceremonies.[3] Other films show poetry, typically translations of the classics, and singing in the form of rhythmic clapping, or dancing to popular tunes like "Yankee Doodle."[4] In her history of Deaf theater, Dorothy Miles describes community performances as descendants of the early "literary societies" founded at schools for the deaf. She claims that the earliest such society is the Clerc Literary Association of Philadelphia, founded in 1865. Gallaudet College founded its literary society in 1874.[5]

Wolf Bragg was popular for his Deaf club performances through the 1930s when he conceived the idea of mounting full-length play productions under the auspices of the Hebrew Association of the Deaf. Using money pooled from friends and fellow aspiring actors, Wolf produced sign language translations of mainstream plays, including *The Monkey's Paw* and *Auf Weidersehen*, both popular with audiences during the years leading up to the Second World War. He rented high school theaters for the evening and printed fliers to distribute at Deaf clubs announcing the place and date of the performances. The plays were wildly popular, filling the theaters with two or three hundred in attendance, in part because Wolf himself was a compelling presence on stage.[6]

Until his departure in 1925, Wolf had attended the New York School for the Deaf at Fanwood and learned the skill of sign storytelling from older students. As in other schools for the deaf at the time, Fanwood had a tradition of performance in the evening hours after classes had ended. Wolf's strong sense of timing and colorfully vivid style of signing could hold an audience for hours. He would entertain audiences of friends at his home with stories cribbed from the *Reader's Digest,* with a favorite being one of a man who at the urging of his wife went on a hiking trip with his best friend, only to find himself the target of a murder planned by his wife and friend, who were having an affair. Without access to movies or to plays, which were not subtitled or captioned in those days, Deaf people were drawn to these informal storytelling events at homes and clubs as well as at plays performed at theaters.[7] Like Yiddish theater aimed at a community both set apart and brought together by its foreign tongue, Deaf theater in New York promised its audience vivid sign language theater, and by all reports, it delivered.

Wolf Bragg's productions brought in Deaf people with little or no experience in acting, with sets designed on a shoestring on borrowed stages. Miles describes Wolf as a "demanding director" who coaxed performances out of fellow Deaf club members. Just as Yiddish theater responded to the growing demand of Jewish immigrants for entertainment in their own language, Deaf theater was designed for Deaf audiences. There was no voiced English translation of these productions because there was no one who needed to hear it. David Lifson describes Yiddish theater as a respite from the difficult lives that Jewish immigrants experienced, and a powerful reminder of what they had left behind in their homelands.[8] In Deaf theater, the homeland was the community and the schools, brought together for a moment in an expression of drama. In the hands of directors like Wolf Bragg, sign language theater was arresting and satisfying.

During this period, Gallaudet College had an active theater; not only was there a dramatic club, where actors were invited to audition, but the college's fraternities and sororities mounted their own plays as well, creating a lively theatrical environment on campus.

Many of these productions featured voice interpretation. In 1932, the Saturday Night Dramatic Club presented *The Curse of the Idol,* featuring an "interpreter." The following year, the club's production listed a student who "interpreted the play for the benefit of the hearing public in the audience." In subsequent years, one or two of the hearing faculty would be listed as an "interpreter" or a "reader."

In the summer of 1941, Eric Malzkuhn was looking for a new production for the Gallaudet Dramatics Club when he read a script of a murder mystery being performed on Broadway, *Arsenic and Old Lace.* Because the rights were not available, Malzkuhn wrote to the producers of the play to ask for an exception. When the producers answered that there could be no simultaneous amateur production while the play was currently on Broadway, Malzkuhn replied that it would not be a simultaneous production because it would be in sign language, and furthermore, it would not be amateur because they were "the best sign language performers in the world." To Malzkuhn's surprise, the producers wrote back and invited the club to perform on the Broadway production's stage during its off night.[9]

Malzkuhn knew that if he was to bring his production to Broadway, he would need a plan for voicing. He selected two of the college's teachers, one who taught mathematics and the other classics, and arranged to put them behind a dark screen to one side of the stage. Though hidden from the audience, their voices would accompany the Deaf actors as they reprised in sign language the comedy of two spinster aunts who poison lonely elderly gentlemen looking to rent a room from them. For one night in May 1942, Eric Malzkuhn and the Dramatics Club found themselves performing on a genuine Broadway stage in front of a hearing audience. After the night was over, the students returned to Gallaudet and the historic event became forever inscribed in the folklore of Deaf theater, and in the black-and-white photographs stored in the club's glass case. For one night, sign language attracted the attention of an almost entirely hearing audience.[10]

It hardly seems compelling theater to have two amateur voices for ten different roles, but voice at the time was augmentive, "interpreted . . . for the benefit of the hearing public in the audience," as the playbill for the *Arsenic and Old Lace* production explained. A few years later, a sign translation of Gilbert and Sullivan's musical *The Mikado* was performed at Gallaudet College, complete with rented wigs and costumes, and ornate sets. It was the most ambitious production by the football-coach-turned-director Ted Hughes. As with *Arsenic and Old Lace,* two teachers from the college provided voice translation, but they were kept off to the side behind a screen, so their uncostumed bodies would not mar the staging of the musical. Their voices were to supplement the play, to help the few hearing members of the audience follow the lines in case the sign language delivery could not be understood. When voice was used in Deaf theater to fill the silence, it was to explain and translate, but it was restrained in ambition.

Voice was intimate, close by and familiar. When Eric Malzkuhn met with the producers of Broadway's *Arsenic and Old Lace*, he brought along a fellow student, Archie Stack, to interpret because he had "a lot of hearing" and used his voice well. From 1930 through 1959, Gallaudet College productions relied on a small group of hearing teachers to read or interpret plays: Elizabeth Benson, a hearing daughter of Deaf parents, was the dean of women at the college, and frequently was called on to interpret not only for productions but also for any interpreting need on the campus. Margaret Yoder taught English and fencing at the college, and voiced for a number of productions, as did Joe Youngs, a hearing graduate student who would later become the superintendent of Maine School for the Deaf. A playbill announcing Gallaudet's production of *Hamlet* in 1958 listed Leonard Siger, on the college's English faculty, as "Reader." He also read for the following year's production of *Othello*. Voice continued to be off-stage and out of sight, and read by "friends" from within the community.

David Hays, then a well-known Broadway set designer, announced in 1966 that he and a consortium of interested individuals and organizations had received funding from the federal government for a new professional company. After a long history of amateur productions on a local scale, the news of a national theater took the Deaf community by surprise, especially since no one had heard of David Hays before. Himself hearing, Hays had no experience with Deaf actors, indeed he had little contact with Deaf people except for an experience watching Deaf people signing in the streets of New York, which struck him as "an oddity." Spurred in part by the success of a Broadway play about Helen Keller, *The Miracle Worker*, Hays began to contemplate the possibilities of a sign language theater for hearing audiences. He began to meet regularly with Edna Levine, a psychologist and mother of two deaf children who had contacts in the Department of Health, Education, and Welfare. Soon she had convinced the office to consider awarding funds for this purpose. Knowing no sign language, Hays traveled to Gallaudet College where he saw a production of *Our Town* and found his perspective changed: "I thought the actors . . . were very moving. There was something about sign language. The quiet communication. The sign and the voice together. The quiet way of speaking . . . it was very touching."[11]

When Bernard Bragg heard plans were afoot to fund a national Deaf theater, he was excited, especially when Edna Levine promised him that she would recommend him to David Hays as someone who could advise him on how to launch this new enterprise. Bernard had grown up in the shadow of his father, Wolf Bragg, and had himself performed in Deaf club theater. As he honed his skills on the stage, he longed for something more. He wanted to perform for larger, even hearing audiences, like the stars he had watched on the stage and on the big screen. He had a difficult relationship with his father who, oddly, did not encourage his ambition to act—instead, he had urged Bernard to go into printing. Bragg wanted to act, but he had ambitions beyond the small and amateur stages of New York Deaf theater.

True to Levine's promise, David Hays contacted Bernard and invited him to help him conceive of the new national theater. The project would begin with a summer school for prospective actors, since Deaf actors accustomed to the community stage needed to be trained for more professional venues. Bernard knew whom he wanted to recommend to David Hays—he had just brought together a group of Deaf actors for a performance at the California Association of the Deaf state convention and the reception from the audience had been tremendous. He told David Hays he knew who would be the best choices for the company—George Johnston was "the perfect Iago" in Gallaudet College's production of *Othello*, as was Howard Palmer in the title role. For the female roles, Bragg wanted his good friend Audree Norton. Hays saw a picture of Audree, who had worked briefly as a model, and immediately agreed. Bragg also thought of the husband-and-wife pair of June and Gilbert Eastman, both from Gallaudet. Charles Corey and Joe Velez were favorite actors in comedic Deaf skits and Bragg decided they should also be included.[12]

From the start, David Hays wanted his new enterprise to be a *professional* theater. Hays had had an illustrious career as set designer, and was himself fully steeped in the Broadway tradition. He would design a theater of the same caliber, with the highest production values. Second, he wanted a *sign language* theater. In a correspondence with Bragg that began in June 1966, Hays explained: "It is my conviction . . . that the manual language theatre can be developed into a startlingly beautiful medium . . . we must evolve methods of performance which will create an art no longer merely a way of bringing theatre to the handicapped, but which is a brilliant new form brought to all of us by the deaf."[13] He wanted a company that would perform in sign language for mainstream hearing audiences. Bragg suggested that the new national theater could explore mime as well, as a way to reach out to hearing audiences. He himself was beginning a career in mime, following in the path of Marcel Marceau under whom he trained.

But Hays was adamant that the theater would not do mime. He intensely disliked "mutism" and the themes of Marceau's continental mime. Hays wanted theater of the kind that he knew best, plays rich in language and dialogue, not mimes trapped in glass boxes and picking flowers in a garden. To him, mime was like puppetry, and his vision of a theater did not include it. To make his vision possible, Hays explained to Bragg that hearing actors would have to be hired as part of the company, to lend their voices to the Deaf actors' performances, to speak the actors' lines as the actors signed them. These would have to be professional actors, not simply readers or even interpreters, because his theater would require those trained in voice. David Hays's vision included hearing actors not disembodied and hidden behind a screen or consigned to the orchestra, but visibly moving across the stage as they voiced the lines of the Deaf actors. Sometimes they would voice in the shadows of Deaf actors; other times they would sign some lines themselves. They would not merely voice the Deaf actors' lines in English, but would themselves be actors and deliver as powerful a performance in voice as in sign.

Hays's conscious choice of sign language over mime has marked Deaf theater from that time to the present in the United States. Elsewhere in the world, including in Moscow and Hong Kong, there are Deaf companies that use mime, not sign language, to reach their audiences. The International Visual Theatre in Paris, too, has experimented with mime and sign language presentations, but since David Hays, American Deaf theater has never seriously considered mime as a medium of communication with hearing audiences; instead it has been primarily a sign language theater.

When the first company of Deaf actors arrived at the Eugene O'Neill Center in Waterford, Connecticut, in the summer of 1967, they were unsure of Hays's novel idea. They considered themselves lucky to be a part of a new professional company, but Deaf theater had never been like this. Deaf theater had always been performed in ASL, and no one had ever come to a Deaf club performance expecting English. When Wolf Bragg staged his sign language production of *Auf Weidersehen* about the Nazi occupation of Germany, the audience came because it followed the tradition of performance in deaf schools and Deaf clubs, that of presenting English-language plays in sign language.

David Hays's idea to put both voice and sign on the stage was remarkable in principle, but as it turned out, fraught with problems. Conflicts quickly arose during the first actors' workshop in the summer of 1967. From the very start, Hays set out to forge together the language of Deaf theater with hearing theater aesthetics and performance values. There would not be the raucous vaudeville that made up amateur Deaf club performances; instead National Theatre of the Deaf (NTD) would be high art. He had some interest in original Deaf productions, but he wanted first to stage well-known plays to prove that his new company could perform them.

To achieve this goal, he brought three New York City directors to Connecticut that summer to work with the Deaf actors: Gene Lasko, who had directed Anne Bancroft in her famous role as Helen Keller's teacher, Annie Sullivan, in *The Miracle Worker;* Joe Layton, a choreographer for Barbra Streisand's Broadway performances; and Joe Chaikin, the director of the radical Open Theatre. There were some Deaf teachers also invited that summer, though not to teach acting or choreography. Instead Robert Panara and

Eric Malzkuhn taught the history of acting, leaving the task of teaching stagecraft to the Broadway directors.

Hays's idea of having Deaf and hearing actors sharing the same stage immediately presented timing issues. For one thing, the leisurely pace that Bernard Bragg used for what he called his "visual vernacular," or "sign-mime"—a blending of mimetic aspects from his training as a mime and his father's vivid sign style—was not suited for the quick tempo that the hearing director, Joe Layton, preferred. In the time that it took Bernard to set up a signed scene, the hearing actor had often finished speaking the line and the stage was left uncomfortably silent. Then as Bernard changed the image, the actor had to quickly chatter through the next line.

Some solutions had to be found. Layton's solution was to order the Deaf actors to reduce the complicated "wordy" signing so the voice would be paced correctly and more pleasingly. Furthermore, he wanted the Deaf actors to move around the stage more. The feet-in-concrete style of community acting, suited for the Deaf club so the audience could watch the signing comfortably, was replaced by a more rapid, and arguably, visually pleasing choreography. Patrick Graybill remembers how much he struggled to keep up. Layton wanted faster and faster choreography, and Graybill tried to compensate. He knew that a moving body makes signing harder for Deaf audiences to understand, so he tried to time his signing during brief pauses on stage so that it would not be lost in the blur of Layton's choreographed movements.

Next to change was the intensely expressive and intimate acting style of Deaf actors. The rubbery faces characteristic of Deaf theater—the wide-open eyes, the exaggerated mouth, the distended wagging tongue, the mobile shoulders, and the shaking head—had to go. The signing on the Deaf actors' hands was "expressive," but their faces seemed grotesque to Hays and other hearing directors. The actors were told to control and choreograph their faces to show more restraint.

The result of this new signing register is evident in the first production of the company on the NBC television show "An Experiment in Television."[14] In Audree Norton's lovely and lyrical rendition of Elizabeth Barrett Browning's "How Do I Love Thee? Let Me Count the Ways," she is seated on a velvet settee in a spotlight. Her face is tightly controlled, with only tiny movements to register small expressions of adoration and affection. Her mouth barely moves; her head turns slowly and her shoulders are even. Instead her hands show the emotion, rising and falling, and then as she reaches the last line of the poem, "I love thee with the breath, Smiles, tears, of all my life!—and, if God choose, I shall but love thee better after death," her face remains unchanged until the end of the poem, signaled by a slow drawing together of her hands in a final clasp of fealty to her beloved.

After their experimental first year, the NTD was ready to mount its touring season in the fall of 1967. They performed for mostly hearing audiences, first near their home in New England, and then in other parts of the country. Two short plays were featured: William Saroyan's *The Man with His Heart in the Highlands,* the wildly funny nonoperatic version of Puccini's *Gianni Schicchi,* and then a collection of poems, including Audree Norton's "How Do I Love Thee?" *Gianni Schicchi* was an immediate hit with the critics, who loved its colorfully outlandish costumes and frantic choreography. Bernard Bragg wore a gaudy harlequin costume complete with prosthetic rubber nose for the title role, and Joe Velez was equally memorable as his assistant. The costumes and sets were far more lavish than any Deaf club theater could ever have hoped to match. As the company traveled to stages around the country, at colleges and universities as well as repertory stages, Deaf audiences found themselves sitting in plush seats in fully professional theaters, and before their eyes was a company of Deaf actors, each of them famous but never before brought together on the same stage. Almost immediately, the Deaf audiences complained about the new theater: Too fast! Incomprehensible! Too elite![15]

Eric Malzkuhn, who had been hired by the NTD in its first two seasons to translate written English script to ASL, remembers that the idea of putting hearing and Deaf actors together on a stage "worked beautifully, and it was terrible." He meant that for *Gianni Schicchi*, it worked beautifully, but the following year, when the company performed Moliere's *Sganarelle*, it became a disaster in Malzkuhn's eyes. The hearing actors were given their own lines to sign, and like *Gianni Schicchi*, there was ambitious choreography, but the Deaf audience was confused about where to look. The actors were signing, yet some were speaking too. The voice actors who would normally be consigned to the background were now more prominent. Tensions mounted as the Deaf actors found themselves competing with hearing actors for the audience's attention.

As the actors tried to resolve the balance between sign and voice, Deaf audiences who came to the first performances of this new theater were surprised that they couldn't understand the performances. Hearing audiences could use sound to track who was speaking on stage, but the Deaf audience couldn't always figure out which actors to look at. Deaf actors moved, but didn't sign. Hearing actors didn't move, but signed. The pacing of Deaf club theater, where the actors behaved as if the stage were a world made up entirely of Deaf people, kept the staging clear to its audiences. But with a new choreography designed for the kind of visual spectacle that hearing audiences were used to, the feel and texture of the NTD was no longer like club theater. Deaf audiences were torn. The NTD had their favorite Deaf actors playing in ensemble, and sign language was displayed favorably to the public, yet it was not the same.

The new use of voice on the public stage foretold a changing order of things, and there was no turning back. By any measure, the NTD was an outstanding success. Clive Barnes, writing for the *New York Times*, called himself charmed by the experiment in sign language, but said that in his opinion, the theater would not work without the use of voice.[16] In subsequent seasons, the NTD staged complex classics, from Dylan Thomas's *Under Milkwood* to Gertrude Stein's *Four Saints in Three Acts*, to prove that the theater had serious ambitions, but both translated poorly into ASL and alienated Deaf audiences.[17]

In Wolf Bragg's time, the audience had been made up of those who came to see mainstream plays in culturally familiar performances. It was segregated theater, and like Yiddish theater of the same period, it was intensely familiar to insiders and by definition, inaccessible to outsiders. Yet within the confines of these expectations, both were fertile theater: They had actors who were popular with their audiences and through their skill, the performances brought to life the language and culture of the community.

The placement of voice on the sign stage was a planned intervention and it changed practices. Beyond making sign language intelligible to hearing audiences, it altered Deaf actors' style of acting. It changed the direction of translation, because the signing now not only needed to match the original English text, but it also had to match the choreography of voiced performance. We tend to think of technology in terms of objects, say a telephone or a computer, but attached to each technology is a body of practices. The technology of writing is not merely the storage of speech in visible form, but an industry of writing: We have writers, editors, and publishers. Beyond these agents, we have paper manufacturers, printers, and book binderies. Howard Becker reminds us that the "genius" of art is not the solitary work that artists do, but includes a "cooperative community" of art brokers and gallery owners, framers, paint and canvas supply houses, and so on, which support, justify, even exalt the work of artists.[18] As Deaf actors moved onto a public stage, the "cooperative" work of actors, directors, and producers put new pressures on signed performance.

When voice became packaged into the bodies of actors and integrated into the performance, it foretold of social change to come.

Sign language theater already had a Deaf audience, but Hays wanted a different audience. He told his company that "our object is not to create just another theatre for the Deaf. Our new theatre is for everybody."[19] Hays astutely recognized that his own growing fascination with sign language was likely to be shared by audiences who were searching for novel kinds of performances. Like him, the public was growing interested in popular kinds of performance, especially of new and exotic groups, and the National Theatre of the Deaf fit the bill. The NTD cleverly marketed Hays's vision of Deaf theater and soon the company had a full schedule of bookings on major stages across the country.

NTD appealed to Deaf performers who had grown restless with the small confines of Deaf club stages and yearned for exposure and fame. Bernard Bragg had dreamed as a child of performing before large audiences but he could not imagine how to do it without voice. When he saw Marcel Marceau command a large audience in San Francisco, he began to think mime might be his vehicle to the public stage. He managed to acquire an invitation to study with Marceau, and after a summer in Paris at his studio, Bernard returned to the United States and tried to build a career as a mime. He landed himself a weekly series on local television called *The Silent Man,* and achieved a small amount of fame. When he could not convince David Hays to try mime in the new NTD, Bernard joined the other Deaf actors and learned to accommodate voice in their acting. Patrick Graybill remembers his time with the NTD as struggling with his fellow actors in the company over the problem of sign translation and timing, but the lure of the professional stage was powerful.

Soon silent sign language theater began to fade away, as did Yiddish theater in the 1940s. Today there is very little theatrical performance in sign language that is not voiced. Sometimes signed poetry or narratives will be performed silently to demonstrate the difficulty of translation into voice, but these are brief, nostalgic performances. Exclusively sign language theater is sometimes found, but audiences are forewarned. There are no more full-length plays only in sign language because today's audiences will not tolerate voicelessness. The comparison with Yiddish theater is apt, but different: While the number of Yiddish speakers in the United States and worldwide has declined, the number of signers of ASL has not—it arguably has increased with more hearing second-language learners of ASL. Yet there is not a very large market for silent sign language theater.

Deaf club theater died because there were no longer Deaf clubs, but instead of going the way of Yiddish theater, sign language theater transformed itself and found a new audience. Audiences for Deaf theater have broadened to include hearing learners of sign language, or those who do not know sign language but are enthralled by its presence. The visibility of sign language, the hint of iconicity, pleases mixed audiences. Simultaneous voice allows them to see sign language "better"—to recognize in a blur of sign delivery the occasional vivid portrayal of objects and states of being.

When NTD's actors performed Layton's choreographed "Three Blind Mice" during the company's staging of *My Third Eye,* the actors held their hands to their chests as paws, and chattered their teeth. Their hands reached back and flicked like tails while they pranced like mice across the stage. The choreography was entirely alien to Deaf club theater: the actors had to "dance" between rows, then rearrange themselves into another grouping, and match their movements to the singing of hearing actors. The performance was guided by voice, which pleased hearing audiences who marvel at how Deaf people can perform in a language both transparent yet foreign.

Deaf club theater did not strive for iconicity; its productions were translations of popular plays, staged to entertain Deaf audiences who wanted to see mainstream plays in their own language.

Wolf Bragg knew how to make signs pleasing to Deaf audiences; he would play with the internal structure of signs to show details of the actors' actions and their reactions to events. But in NTD, the emphasis was on sign transparency: Bernard Bragg remembers Gene Lasko asking the actors to "stretch out their signs" to make them more iconic and thus more recognizable to the audience. The actors should not simply sign that "the arm was bloody," but actually hold up the arm, and slowly show the blood flowing down the arm and droplets dripping off the arm.

Soon after, voice as a technology began to be deployed in arenas other than the theater—in education, social service, government, and the workplace. Several years after the NTD's inaugural season in 1966, a series of federal laws were passed guaranteeing access to the deaf and disabled. Section 501 of the Rehabilitation Act of 1973 prohibits discrimination against the disabled in any federal agency. Section 504 of the same act expands the protection to include any federally supported program. Shortly after the passage of Public Law 94-142, also known as the Education for All Handicapped Children Act of 1975, public school districts were required to admit and provide education to any deaf and disabled children. As deaf children and adults moved out of segregated schools into new public arenas, the workplace and the integrated school, interpreters not only signed for them, but provided voice as well, to translate signs into spoken English. Whereas public school education had been typically limited to deaf or hard-of-hearing children who could speak for themselves, schools now provided voice interpreters who spoke for students if they could not do so themselves.

The expansion of disability rights through the next two decades culminated in the far-reaching Americans with Disabilities Act of 1990, which guaranteed access in commercial spaces as well as public ones. Television manufacturers are now required to install a captioning decoder chip in all televisions larger than thirteen inches, enabling nearly every television in the United States to provide captions on the screen. Hotels have to be accessible to the disabled, including by providing televisions equipped with decoder chips. Deaf people who wish to attend union meetings or work-place training can request interpreters who can both sign and voice, gaining them access in expression as well as in information. Unlike during the International Typographical Union's chapel meetings of the 1940s and 1950s, when Deaf workers relied on hard-of-hearing coworkers to interpret for them, the American Postal Workers' Union today provides interpreters for its Deaf union members. Participation in public government also expanded under the new law. Los Angeles County has a staff legal advocate whose responsibility is to meet with every deaf or hard-of-hearing person who enters the legal system and determine their communi-cative needs. If voice as well as signing are needed, the advocate arranges for an interpreter to be present at all legal matters involv-ing the individual. Giving voice to a deaf defendant or petitioner has become an expanded legal right only recently. Hospitals can be sued for failing to provide interpreters when medical information is gathered from a deaf patient at the time of admission.

Deaf people's use of voice has not only deployed human actors and interpreters in the service of Deaf individuals, but also led to the design of new types of machines. In 1985, the California Asso-ciation of the Deaf (CAD) and the Greater Los Angeles Association of the Deaf (GLAD), an agency providing social services to deaf people, petitioned the California Utilities Commission to provide telephone access to deaf and hard-of-hearing residents of the state. Arguing that any public utility should be fully inclusive, the orga-nizations demanded that the commission provide free-of-charge teletext machines so that deaf people could access the telephone lines to do real-time exchange of text messages, just as phone com-panies at that time provided telephones free of charge for the hear-ing. Furthermore, they wanted the commission to support tele-phone access between individuals who had the text machines and those who did not.

Local Deaf agencies in California had been experimenting with using hearing operators who would read incoming teletype calls to a caller who did not have teletype equipment. The CAD wanted the service funded by telephone subscription fees and expanded to twenty-four hours, seven days a week to any citizen living in California. Using the relay, Deaf people could call hearing relatives, shop owners, doctors, catalog companies, work supervisors, and others over the telephone. The utilities commission agreed, and in 1987, inaugurated the new service, in which calls to and from the operator were free of charge, and the telephone toll charge was as if the Deaf caller had dialed the hearing caller directly.[20] To pay for the cost of distributing equipment and hiring relay operators, the commission created a surcharge added to all phone bills. The technology provided voice for Deaf consumers to use and to exploit in conjunction with other technologies.

Quickly recognizing that relay services could be lucrative given the subsidy, telephone companies aggressively bid for the right to offer them. And Deaf people, no longer limited to borrowing the voices of neighbors and relatives, clamored for the service, causing the demand to skyrocket. In the first month in California, 50,000 calls were relayed after the new service was inaugurated. Five years later, the service spread through the rest of the country and there were 315,000 calls per month. By 2001, there were approximately 51,000 calls *a day* to relay centers throughout the United States.[21] Text relay services are tightly mediated, with the operator speaking the text lines slowly and limiting interruptions from the hearing caller, but the service has established the principle of public access for deaf telephone users, and is now commonplace throughout the United States. To make it more convenient to use and remember, many states have converted the toll-free number that callers use to reach the relay center to a simple three-digit one, 711.

To handle the volume of calls, a telephone carrier offering relay services may employ as many as one hundred relay operators during the peak hours of 10:00 a.m. to 3:00 p.m., weekdays. Depending on the carrier, the actual location of the operators may not even be within the state where the call is made; Sprint employs operators throughout the country and has centers located in California, South Dakota, and Texas. As the operator comes on line and identifies her or his gender and operator number (for example, "Operator 456F" for a female operator), the caller gives the phone number to dial and waits for the operator to connect with the other party. Throughout the conversation, the operator maintains as strict a mediator role as possible: no personal conversations should take place between the operator and the deaf caller, nor should the operator engage in overmediation and try to respond on behalf of either party. Voice relay is expected to be impersonal and objective, with the identity of the operator limited to the gender and code. Whereas thirty years ago Deaf people asked neighbors, friends, coworkers, and children to make telephone calls on their behalf, calls are now made by hearing strangers whose identity and location are never known.

The blending of human voice and intelligent machines has moved to the next level with *video* relay services, which use cameras and the Internet to link Deaf signing "callers" to a live interpreter. The Deaf caller goes to a website where the image of a sign language interpreter appears on the screen. Once the interpreter sees the video image of the Deaf caller as well, the call is initiated and the telephone transaction takes place in sign language and the operator's voice using cameras. Video relay calls likewise use interpreters in remote locations, and the role of the interpreter is strictly limited to transmitting language between the two callers. The service has expanded to hospitals, where instead of arranging for a live interpreter for Deaf patients who arrive at the hospital, the staff wheels in a video monitor with a camera attached to a high-speed phone line. The video interpreting service is dialed up, and an interpreter working out of her home in another state comes on the monitor and interprets for the Deaf patient.

Voice can also be contained in small portable machines. Deaf people can own text pagers that convert written text to speech using a fairly realistic mechanical voice for the purpose of leaving voice messages with hearing callers. Voice recognition software is also now being used for remote live voice translation. The voice of the speaker in a public speaking situation is transmitted to an operator and a small desktop computer via a high-speed telephone line where it is translated into text using voice recognition software, then transmitted back to the location of the speaker where it is projected onto a screen as English subtitles or captions. To compensate for the relatively high error rate of voice recognition software, trained operators monitor incorrect word choices and type in corrections. In this configuration, the divide between the human and the mechanical becomes blurred because the "interpreter" is never actually seen but is mediated entirely by machine. In essence, as the human-to-human interaction in voice translation is broken down, voice reaches a new level of alienation, where its translation to text is never completely human. Conspiring with the arts, the public utilities, the government, and private industry, Deaf people have given themselves the ability to speak in new ways, even as they do not themselves produce voice in their own bodies.

Far from being an unknown entity, voice is a very serious matter to Deaf people. In his autobiography, *Lessons in Laughter*, Bernard Bragg tells how he had to be taught how to laugh because his untutored laughter was too strange to the hearing ear. Deaf people who are self-conscious about their own voices will insist on hearing people's voice interpretation of their language. For short interactions, such as an order in a restaurant or a chance encounter with a hearing person, Deaf people will use writing to communicate because to attempt to use an unmodulated voice is risky. Joseph Grigeley, a Deaf artist, memorialized his many written encounters with hearing friends and strangers into an unusual art form titled White Noise, once on exhibit at the Whitney Museum of American Art.[22] Scraps of paper saved over the years, ranging from instructions to philosophical ruminations, were wallpapered on a curved surface, showing interactions preserved in writing. For most of their history, Deaf people in the United States have managed their use of voice, either by using others' voices or through writing; in this sense, technological transformation of voice is not new to the community.

When faculty members Elizabeth Benson and Edward Scouten voiced behind a screen off-stage for Gallaudet College's 1947 production of *The Mikado*, they were there because the hearing faculty wanted to hear the lines of Gilbert and Sullivan said out loud and not because they didn't understand the language of the production. At that time, many hearing faculty at Gallaudet were fluent signers before teaching at the college. A number had Deaf parents, or had come to the profession because of another family connection to deafness. Yet even with hearing faculty, the campus was segregated and limited to those who knew sign language well. Interpretation, while available, was not used on the scale it is today. When Benson and Scouten were at Gallaudet, both were the only interpreters the campus had or needed, because the contexts for using interpreters were few. Within the campus, there were many signers, but outside the campus there were very few. Today there are many more signers outside the group, and for those who do not sign, there are technologies to mediate interaction.

Today interpreting has become highly professionalized and has reached a massive scale. The largest interpreter referral agencies employ long rosters of interpreters and send them out to a variety of settings, from educational to social service to corporate and legal as well as personal. One large agency serving the western United States has 143 interpreters on its roster available for assignment; of this number, twelve are employed full-time. As an estimate of the demand, interpreters in San Diego work a combined 234,000 hours a year. At an average of twenty dollars an hour, total payments to interpreters easily exceed $1 million a year—for one metropolitan region. Viewed nationally, a conservative estimate of payments made to sign language interpreters must be at least $100 million. Deaf adults and children routinely use the voices of professional interpreters—to talk to their doctors, to talk to their teachers and to teach themselves, to make their weddings accessible to hearing family and friends, and for nearly every other aspect of their lives.

Voice can simplify tasks for Deaf people. Instead of writing out their wishes, Deaf people can use voice interpreters to speak simultaneously as they sign. Instead of faxing to businesses or visiting them personally, Deaf people can remain at home and use the relay service to call and inquire about their products. But technology is about rearrangement and replacement; as new practices are adopted, older practices decline. Deaf actors can perform before new audiences with voice accompanying them on the stage, but they have to alter their style of signing. Where once they occupied the stage entirely and without compromise, they now have to share the stage with voice actors and accommodate the constraints of voiced performance. The technology of voice brought Deaf actors to the public stage, but shortly after, silent Deaf theater began its decline, and for all purposes is today only a nostalgic theater.

Where once voice belonged to people who hear and Deaf people were said to be "mute," over the years Deaf people have assumed greater ownership of voice. Managing the technology of voice is a means by which Deaf people have carved out a public space for themselves in American life. As their sign language moved into public places, voice moved with it. In the process, Deaf people have made themselves less a secret community, and more a public one—at a cost.

6

Anxiety of Culture

Silent Deaf theater never needed to give "lessons" to hearing people. The only hearing people who came were those who already knew the language and were related to Deaf people either by family or by some other intimate relation. The aim of Deaf theater was to entertain Deaf people, and to translate the world into their own terms. Their theaters were private and out of sight of the mainstream. Deaf people lived their lives outside the public glare, in borrowed and temporary spaces, figuratively mute as well as invisible. Sign language was mysterious and obfuscating, not to be readily understood. The history of how sign language came to be, how the different groups of deaf people came together, and how they lived their lives, were known only by those in the community.

But once the actors of the National Theatre of the Deaf mounted the stage in the fall of 1967, their language and way of life suddenly became public and enormously visible. Hearing theater critics wrote about their signing, and hearing audiences applauded their signed performances. Even Deaf people noticed the actors' signs, especially when they complained that the signing was too fast. Once seen by others, the actors turned their lives into material for the stage and began to objectify themselves. The fact of their

123

signing and their not speaking became a matter of public curiosity and an object of discussion. Where silence was once not noticed, it was now a commodity, and for that matter, made even more emphatic by voice interpretation. Signing was the manner of performing, and it was itself the performance. Astonished, the Deaf actors began to look at their own hands, and literally began to watch themselves sign.

Outside the world of theater, a storm was gathering. While the NTD actors were experimenting with what to show and say about their language and culture on stage, William Stokoe, a hearing scholar, and his Deaf colleagues at Gallaudet College, Carl Croneberg and Dorothy Casterline, had just published a new sign language dictionary.[1] In this dictionary, signs were listed not by their translations in English, as had previous dictionaries of sign languages, but by their internal structure: the combination of handshapes, locations or where the signs were produced on or around the body, and the type of movement. This was a first true dictionary of a sign language written, as the authors say, "on linguistic principles," or on its own terms, rather than by derivation or translation through another language.

Science and art had come together in a brilliant confluence of discovery: that sign languages are human languages, and could be analyzed and understood as any other language in the world. Sign language could be codified in a dictionary and performed on a Broadway stage, both powerfully legitimizing acts. It should have been a moment of sheer exhilaration, but instead the community was stricken by a profound anxiety.

Instead of praise, the dictionary drew bitter criticism and anger. Gilbert Eastman, a drama professor at Gallaudet at the time, remembered some thirty-five years later, at a conference honoring the eightieth birthday of William Stokoe, that when he first heard of the dictionary, he "vehemently despised" Stokoe for having done such a thing. How dare a hearing person write such a dictionary of Deaf people's language? How dare he represent his language in this bizarre form—as a collection of nonsensical symbols, squiggles, and invented vocabulary? Stokoe had invented a new word, "chereme," to describe the smaller parts of a sign, drawing from the Latinate *cher* to mean "gesture" because he could not find a vocabulary ideal for his purposes. He added "tab" for location, "dez" for handshape, and "sig" for movement.[2] Eastman was incensed at the audacity of what Stokoe had done. He was an outsider, trampling through the language for gain and profit. Stokoe had been hired to teach English literature at the college, but somehow had become sidetracked; supposedly he taught Chaucer by day, but in his spare time, he had managed to convince two Deaf colleagues to join him in a "vanity" project.

In the early 1960s, structural linguistics, which had originated in Europe as part of a movement to compare languages of the world, was gaining a foothold in American colleges and universities as an academic discipline.[3] In this approach to language study, languages were described according to the design of their sound structures, the organization of their morphemes and vocabulary, and their sentence structures. By coding these structures, languages could be more easily compared, and histories of language families could be tracked over time. Stokoe was convinced he could show that the same structures can be found in sign languages.

Because structural linguistics relied heavily on the description of the sound system, Stokoe needed to show that signs could be organized in the same way: as having smaller units that are assembled together in rule-governed combinations. His dictionary was both analysis and product; he demonstrated the linguistic principles by inventing an entirely new system for representing signs. But strangely, instead of being praised for his efforts, he was reviled and ridiculed. A decade later, the dictionary would turn out to be the beginning of a new generation of sign language studies that would change how we understand the human capacity for language and thought.[4] Today there are university laboratories throughout the world devoted to the study of sign language, but in 1965, the dictionary received little scientific recognition.

Shortly after the introduction of the dictionary, the initial reaction of incredulity had transformed into a massive anxiety and confusion around sign language, both in the Deaf community and outside. The first struggle was to come to an agreement about a new name for the sign language. For the older generation the language of Deaf people in America was simply called "the sign language." Until then in everyday talk and throughout all official publications of Gallaudet College and the National Association of the Deaf, there was no other name than "the sign language" when referring to how Deaf people communicate. Stokoe and his colleagues, in the tradition of comparative linguistics, decided to alter "the sign language" to "the American sign language," as a way to distinguish the American language from other sign languages of the world. Shortly after, the label shortened and became fully capitalized and the language was called "American Sign Language." But even among those who embraced the idea of American Sign Language as a distinct language, it was not yet clear how to talk about it as a language.

Lou Fant published a new sign language book in 1972, using a name he had invented for the language, a collapsing of words into one: "Ameslan." In the introduction, he explained that as a hearing child of deaf parents, he had grown up learning the language at the hands of his deaf parents. He believed that unlike English, "Ameslan" was communicated visually, not linearly, and that the "pure" form of the language had no fingerspelling; instead, it relied on images created through signs to build sentences.[5] We know today that fingerspelling is very much a part of ASL, having a history as long as if not longer than American Sign Language.[6] At the time, however, Fant wanted to demonstrate the uniqueness of the sign language, perhaps by distancing it from English—yet at the cost of an incorrect observation. After a short life, the name "Ameslan" was dropped in favor of "ASL," perhaps because Ameslan seemed less like a scientific term.

Instead of relieving the anxiety, each new label seemed only to increase it, provoking heated debate and ideological clashes within the community. At the start, the term "American Sign Language" or "ASL" was denied by many. Instead of embracing a legitimization of the language they had used for their entire lives, they were suspicious of it. Instead of seeing American Sign Language as a designation of one of many sign languages around the world, they worried more about the claim that ASL was separate from English.

Here class divisions began to manifest themselves in the debate. In their eagerness to portray ASL as different from English, linguists during the early years may have labored too hard to make it seem more exotic, more unusual than it really was. Among the educated elite of the Deaf community, graduates of Gallaudet College and their faculty, many, like Gilbert Eastman, were openly derisive. Even if they were willing to agree that ASL was different from English, ASL wasn't the language *they* used. Their signing was English influenced and educated; ASL was used by the less educated in the Deaf community, the "grassroots," a class term used to refer to those who attend Deaf clubs, work at lower-paying trades, and never went to college. The educated elite used English in their signing, as evidenced by the greater use of fingerspelling and the fact that their sentences followed English word order more closely.

Did this development in naming the language represent a new kind of stigma, making Deaf people different in yet another respect? They were already different, and now as users of a different language, were they carrying an additional burden of strangeness? What, they asked, was the nature of this language with the new label? What made it deserving of a new designation? These questions were spawned in part by Deaf people struggling to confront others' ideas about the poverty of their sign language. Having been told many times by the more powerful science of others that sign languages were nothing more than imperfect systems, they were suddenly required to reconcile two disparate notions: that sign language had linguistic structure and that it was not a language.

James Woodward suggested that the form of signing that many of the Gallaudet elite described themselves as using could be called "Pidgin Sign English" (PSE).[7] He had noticed that signers changed word order or added more fingerspelled words when in the presence of English users. Because the communicative setting involved power imbalances between Deaf signers and hearing signers who were native users of English, he borrowed the term "pidgin" from spoken language study to describe the moment of language use when speakers of one language changed their vocabulary and grammar to accommodate speakers of a different language. Stokoe described the language situation at Gallaudet and other places as similar to a "diglossic" continuum where sign language varied from more like ASL to more like English.[8]

Instead of easing tensions, Stokoe and Woodward's attempts at describing sign language structure and form seemed only to increase them. The comparison of sign language with the spoken language pidgins of the Caribbean and South Pacific exacerbated the sense of strangeness and "otherness" that linguists brought to the community. True, the comparison to similar language situations elsewhere in the world drew ASL more into the class of world languages, but the vocabulary of science, including words like "diglossia" and "pidgin," was not always reassuring. Hidden seams of prejudice against different styles of signing began to be exposed among both Deaf and hearing people.

Adding fuel to the fire was a growing movement in schools and programs for the deaf that ran counter to the growth of sign language studies in colleges and universities. With the goal of teaching English to deaf students, committees of teachers met to invent vocabularies of signs in which ASL signs were modified and new signs invented. New signs were believed to be needed because ASL was not thought to have equivalents to English words.[9] The ASL sign PANTS, used to refer to any category of pants, from jeans to trousers, was modified as two new signs, one with the P handshape for PANTS, and the handshape J to mean JEANS. A further example was a modification of pronouns in ASL, which are gender-free and involve pointing in space. Because the signs did not mark gender, new signs were invented for "she," "he," "her," and "him." In addition, ASL does not inflect TO-BE, so the teachers proposed separate signs for "am," "is," "was," "were," as well as "be" and "been." This language engineering by committee brought the debate over ASL to a fevered pitch, as Deaf people, wary of educators' attempts to modify sign language, protested the efforts.

The fact that many Deaf people were involved in these attempts to "improve" ASL—or replace it in schools with a "better" option—shows how deeply conflicted the community found itself. Just as ASL was gaining academic credence, the movement in support of signed English likewise rose in prominence.[10] The community had long invested in written English and competence in speech as paths to advancement within a hearing world, and using signed English seemed like a reasonable extension of the same belief. But the shift to recognizing ASL and Deaf culture caused conflict in the community because it meant that what had traditionally been devalued suddenly became valued.

There had long been threats on sign language from oralists, but their threats were to banish sign language altogether. Now outsiders were threatening not to eliminate, but to name, describe, modify, even to promote sign language, albeit in a different form. One would expect the recognition of ASL to be celebrated; it instead caused conflict and anxiety. The more that linguists argued that ASL was different and independent from English, the more the community agonized over whether it made sense to be "for" ASL, because what would that make them? It might mean becoming something they didn't yet understand. Did the new move to language legitimacy threaten a move toward more "difference," isolation, and stigmatization? Many thought so. Others embraced the new rhetoric, because it offered the possibility of rethinking the politics of language between deaf and hearing people.

This conflict and anxiety can be understood as the struggle of moving into a public sphere, where the age-old arguments over identity and language now had new stakes. The NTD represented an opening up of the community to the public, requiring the actors to reveal what had once been private as newly public. As Deaf actors struggled to decide which parts of themselves they wanted to use on the stage, the Deaf community battled over what to name their language, what to call their practices, and how to present themselves in a public language. It could be said that once exposed to the bright lights of science and the public's interest, Deaf language and culture irreversibly changed. They certainly became more self-conscious, more deliberate, and more animated, in order to take their place on a larger, more public stage.

When the Deaf community went public, it was clear that there was a great deal of work ahead. Much would have to be rethought and redone. There was a new concept not only of "language," but also of "culture." Deaf people's community life was described variously as "our ways of doing things," "our common beliefs," or "deaf world," but not yet as a culture. With the introduction of the concept came the difficulty of matching science to the everyday lives of Deaf people: What is a "culture"? How does one determine the boundaries of such an entity? Are Deaf people a distinct culture? Or are they more appropriately identified as a subculture of hearing culture? Was there one culture or more? If the culture entailed use of ASL, where did orally trained or late learners of ASL fit in? Where should hearing people be placed in the organization of the community?

Issues of "membership" became the focus of the discussion, and anxiety crept into the debate. How could one become a "member of the Deaf community"? Are there recent arrivals, late arrivals, or nonarrivals? How much knowledge is needed for membership? Scientists offered definitions of "culture" less focused on membership, but the literature did not relieve the anxiety.

The idea of a language and culture promised a great deal; it promised equity and opportunity. If a community had its own language, and its own culture, it could claim certain rights equivalent to those claimed by minority groups. It could claim an interest in affairs having to do with deaf children and adults. It could realign the relationship of Deaf people to their schools, since now, as a distinct cultural group, they had an independent interest in the school curriculum. Furthermore, as the notion of culture was gaining a great deal of attention in the public—especially as issues of race and ethnicity moved to the forefront of American life during the 1960s and 1970s—the headiness of the idea of culture brought with it the sobering realization of how to enact it, how to translate it into terms for everyday life. And on this point, Deaf people disagreed. They debated among themselves such questions as: "What is ASL?" "Who is Deaf?" and "Is there a Deaf culture?" all of which were emotional political issues. The convention of using the capitalized *D*eaf to emphasize the *cultural* drew even more attention to the description of Deaf cultural practices, but *whose* practices and *which* practices counted?[11]

In this moment of transition, the arts, including the NTD, played a role by modeling for the public a new mixing of languages and practices. ASL poets and storytellers of the 1970s and 1980s were among the more influential forces in guiding the community's transition through this period of public debate. Some were in some way connected to the NTD. Dorothy Miles and Patrick Graybill performed in the first few seasons of the NTD. Ella Lentz attended summer school at NTD, and then worked with Dorothy Miles, performing Dorothy's poetry in public while she began writing her own original pieces. Clayton Valli never had contact with the NTD; in fact, he had developed much of his first poetry on his own while working as a teacher of the deaf in Nevada. Debbie Rennie performed in Rochester, New York. There were also inventive and popular ASL storytellers, including Sam Supalla, Ben Bahan, and Ted Supalla. All of these storytellers and poets consciously created performances that emphasized ASL as content and form. In this respect, they departed from the earlier generation of sign language poets like Merv Garretson, Robert Panara, and Willard Madsen, who came from the generation that called their language "the sign language."

Dorothy Miles, or Dot as she liked to call herself, was one of the first poets of this generation of ASL poetry. Through her poetry, from her earliest to her last contributions, she modeled a transformation in the relationship between ASL and English. Miles was British-born, and as she recounts in "Biographies" in the NTD's first original production, *My Third Eye*, she stopped hearing at the age of nine after a long childhood illness. After attending deaf schools in England where she learned her first sign language, British Sign Language, she came to Gallaudet in 1958 and while there, became actively involved in theater. She played mostly supporting roles, until her last year at Gallaudet when she played opposite Phyllis Frelich in *Medea*, and caught the attention of her acting colleagues as a promising talent. Though dedicated, she was not yet a powerful actor, so when the National Theatre of the Deaf opened, she was not on the original roster. She joined the company first as a wardrobe mistress, then in the following season she was hired for a role in the lead play, Dylan Thomas's *Under Milkwood*.[12]

In this production, Miles was an intense presence, and she brought a great deal of creative energy to the company. In addition to performing, she helped to translate scripts, and found herself moving between English and sign language. She directed one segment of *My Third Eye*, "Side Show," and contributed poetry for the company's offshoot Little Theatre of the Deaf, aimed at a younger audience of children and teenagers. As she explains in a videotape of her work while she was visiting at the Salk Institute in La Jolla, California, she had experimented with writing poetry mostly "about nature and love" ever since she was a child, but her poetry began to take shape and to undergo deep changes while she was at the NTD.[13]

At first, Miles found her colleagues not "particularly impressed by my 'new technique' of combining spoken poetry with sign language." She had experimented matching signs with words to try and create poetry that would be equally spare. Her classic haiku "The Seasons," written around 1970, illustrates her early experiments with this technique:[14]

Spring
Sunshine, borne on breeze
among singing trees, to dance
on rippled water.

In the first line of the first verse, she signs SUN, BREEZE, AMONG SINGING TREES, then for the second line, DANCE ON RIPPLED-WATER, SPARKLING-WATER. The lines were both literal and interpretive, using the signed prepositions AMONG and ON as well as using signs to evoke vivid images of the wind whistling through the trees and the sunlight rippling on the water. Hers was a simultaneous "translation" in which the English is preserved as well as in ASL, both matched in timing and line structure. This is in fact typical of the last generation of sign language poetry, in that it attempts to maintain fidelity to the English text, but present signing in lyrical form. In this case, the signing followed the sequence of English words, retaining them as the signs translated the meaning.

Whereas other Deaf poets wrote poetry in English about deaf themes, as in Merv Garretson's "To a Deaf Child," Miles's poetry was beginning to experiment with the evocative power of signs themselves, how they could make images as well as translate the poem.[15] In her haiku, she signs how the breeze moves among the tree branches, but also separately signs AMONG and SINGING. Garretson used traditional verse structure, and carefully planned the rhyming of English words in the lines of the poem. Miles's experiment at this point became less traditional, but she still was faithful to translating between English and ASL.

Later, while developing material for a company performance aimed at children and teenagers, Miles tried a different tack and wrote a poem "that is written for the sign language." As she explains: "When I first wrote that poem, I signed I CAN HOLD A TREE IN PALM OF MY HAND. Those were my words." She had, as in the earlier poem, translated the words in each line from English into ASL, matching signs to words, but then when "I showed [the poem] to my great friend Remy Charlip . . . he told me, 'Why not start with the image? Don't start with the words, I CAN, because that's not necessary in the poem.' I read through it and realized he was right so I eliminated all the I CAN's from it so that I *showed* I could instead of *saying* I could."[16] The "showing" was the use of ASL to create imagery.

As she continued to experiment, she began to integrate the two languages more deeply, delving even further into their structural differences, revealing how different the languages were though they were matched in time line for line.

Language for the Eye

Hold a tree in the palm of your hand,
or topple it with a crash.
Sail a boat on finger waves,
or sink it with a splash.
From your finger tips see a frog leap,
at a passing butterfly.
The word becomes the picture in this language for the eye.

Here, Miles signs TREE with her left palm below her right elbow, and then allows the hand and arm to "topple." She deftly switches from TREE to BOAT-SAILING-ACROSS-FINGER-WAVES (all as one sign), with the left hand mimicking the rolling motion of waves. The BOAT then sinks, and the two hands together form SPLASH. Returning to English, Miles signs FROM FINGER-TIPS SEE FROG LEAP PASS BUTTERFLY. She pauses and then signs the last line of the verse: WORD BECOMES PICTURE IN THIS LANGUAGE FOR EYE. Though literal, she shifts her eye gaze to move between signs, to show the transition from "word" to "picture."

After five years with the company, Miles left the NTD and began to travel around the country, including stays at the Salk Institute, then a center for the early work on American Sign Language, where she interacted with sign language linguists. There she became more reflective about how she used language in her poetry. No longer content to do conventional verse, she experimented even further with her work, pushing the boundaries she had maintained between the two languages. The result was an explosive poem aptly titled "Defiance." By way of introduction, she explains: "Last summer when I knew I was leaving the NTD, I went through a really big change in my life and soon I was writing things that I really felt were poetry. And one of them was the expression of my grief and anger at separating from the NTD, and it came out in sign language and English and it's called, "If I were I . . ."[17]

Defiance

If I were I
I would not say those pleasant things that *I* say;
I would not smile and nod my head
When you say
No!
I would not bear, restrain, repress my disagreement,

But argue every point to puncturing—
Then smile,
If I were I.

What is remarkable about the poem is the way that she pushes the structural possibilities of ASL further than she ever had before. She does not simply sign the lines, but manipulates the signs themselves to create new forms of meaning. Conventionally, the line would be signed: IF I TRADE I, or "If I were to replace myself with a different I," but she inserts a sign that is not translated into English at all: HYPOCRITE. She signs IF followed by the sign HYPOCRITE, and then the next sign, I, is signed directly *on* the handshape for HYPOCRITE, which would be best translated as: "If I were to replace my hypocritical self with a different I." Following this type of "portmanteau" of juxtaposing one sign on another—done only with artistic license, not in everyday language—she then signs TRADE followed by I. Abandoning literal translation, Miles has gone beyond the English to create a line in sign poetry that has meaning above and beyond the words. Where her poetry had previously matched the two languages faithfully in translation and structure, here she tips the scale in favor of ASL. The Deaf audience is surprised by the invention, and pleased. In the meantime, listeners of English hear a well-designed poem in English, but it is not exactly the same one that signers see.

Miles's journey in her own poetry, from what could be called "matched" translations to "parallel" translations, reflects a deepening sense of sign language as a medium for cultural expression and a separation in Deaf people's own minds between the two languages. A poetry was born that was strongly "sign-centered," that is, unabashedly independent of English and in the words of Michael Davidson, "not phonocentric."[18] In her performances, Miles sought to reach out to the Deaf community by emphasizing during her performance elements that were private and special to the group. The sign HYPOCRITE in Miles's poem is not spoken in English, and is understood only by those who know the language and the special mode of sign invention.

With Miles came a generation of poets and performers who expanded on her example: Patrick Graybill, Ella Lentz, Debbie Rennie, and Clayton Valli created poetry that was signed first, and translated into English at a later time or not at all. In all their public performances, they sought to celebrate the potential of ASL, to use signs and forms that were both familiar and new. Ella Lentz in "Eye Music" borrows the all-familiar experience (to deaf people) of watching telephone lines dance through space while riding in a car, and incorporates it into a poem about the internal music of watching visual patterns.[19] Davidson describes these sign poets as "using ASL as a powerful counter-discourse to phonocentric models for literature. In their work, 'performing the text' means utilizing ASL signing to establish community (the Deaf audience understands a sign's multiple meanings) and politicize the occasion (the hearing audience cannot rely on acoustic prosodic models)."[20]

Their performances offered for the Deaf community, at a time when it was arrested with anxiety, a vision of how to represent themselves in a discourse of language and culture. The poetry spoke of independence and equity, with presentations that were equated with, but not subservient to, English. Gradually the poetry and the performances of equally inventive and skilled ASL storytellers like Sam Supalla and Ben Bahan became a new standard for public performance, showing that ASL should become the name of the language of the community, because it had such rich potential.

Today, sign poetry, indeed all forms of signed performance, is very popular with audiences. Poetry readings have been scheduled across the country in various venues. Many sign poets have "published" their poetry on videotape, for sale to students of sign language and other members of the community. Chris Krentz sees a large shift to film and video publishing for art forms in the community, and argues that the trend may have mixed consequences.[21]

The immediate, audience-based performances of the Deaf clubs where recordings were rarely made have been supplanted by commercial videos of signed performances that can be purchased for home and classroom viewing. Krentz wonders if the change from large auditoriums to small, intimate domestic and educational spaces will affect sign poetry and make it more formal and stilted, transforming what used to be "oral" and face-to-face into something more like written poetry, to be viewed over and over again for formal purposes.

It may be that one consequence of the trend to video is that it has allowed sign poetry to develop into new, more reflective forms. Peter Cook, a Deaf poet, and Kenneth Lerner, a hearing person who performs with Cook, use video extensively as a medium for developing their poetic text. Their work is perhaps more free from the anxiety that earlier ASL poets felt. No longer required to establish ASL as a separate language in the public mind or to be advocates of ASL because the label is no longer as provocative as it was when Dot Miles was performing, the poets playfully tease the audience about ASL:[22]

Lerner: Ok, now, I have a confession.
Cook: What did you say? You have a confession?
Lerner: A confession. I've been doing some research. I've been studying; I've been chatting with experts. I'm sorry to tell you that I've learned that ASL is not a language. When compared with English, it stinks.
Cook: That's not true!
Lerner: ASL sucks!
Cook: That's not right!
Lerner: [*Begins to mime apes.*]
Cook: [*Pretends to take a swing at Lerner.*]
Lerner: Anyway. . .

Cook: Where did you learn this "research"? From them? [*points to audience*]

Lerner: People here? No! My audiologist told me.

The exchange segues into a particularly vivid performance about a bird who flies into the side of a house, and because the poem is so obviously about the potential of ASL to portray in detail the feathered characteristics of the bird, its flight and its eventual demise, the exchange is only tongue-in-cheek. During the routine between the two poets, the audience knowingly laughs at them, because at this time, the community has come full circle. ASL is not as volatile a label as it was nearly thirty years ago, and at this time, there is ease and familiarity instead of anxiety and hostility among both Deaf audiences and hearing audiences. Shortly following this exchange, Cook and Lerner set up the next poem, and take yet another cultural swipe:

Lerner: Okay now. Now that you understand a different perspective, we're going to show you a weird poem.

Cook: The poem is called "e=mc²," or "Relativity."

Lerner: And please . . . don't. . . try. . . to understand this poem.

The poem is vaguely about traveling through the universe, alternating between earth and space, the simultaneous voiced translation provided by Lerner as odd as the signed performance by Cook:

E=MC² (or Relativity)

E and Ed, man's sperm equals a monster, M, C, crunch crunch.
Spit 'em out, squared man
Right side up, upside down, right side up
He goes into a strange kind of a landscape,
Shaped kinda like this, so it goes
Up and over and under and down and
Up and over and under and down.

And off the side, he is falling.
Snow, snow, snow heavy snow, pushing down
Until it's pushed back up in the sky
Snow rising into clouds, swirling from below the sun
Burns a hole right through above the earth
Rotating, the pilot blasts off, out over the earth
Through clouds, through clouds, through clouds, and then out,
    up
Upside down, right side up, and while he answers the phone

At the conclusion of the piece, the poets sign *backwards* and match it in spoken words:

Man squared crunch see a monster sperm man equals egg e,
Poem understand try don't please and etip etilair
Which is squared c m equal e.

Cook and Lerner have freed themselves from the obligation to make sense, to present a message, or to do ASL poetry in the conventional sense. Though they do poetry that tells messages—indeed, poetry in the sense that Dot Miles meant it, full of knowledge about the language and its political situation—they also experiment and draw attention to the very act of ASL poetry itself. At every turn during their performances, their audiences understand what they are doing. They laugh and cheer at every pretense of the poets. Sign poetry has reached a point where it no longer needs to teach or justify itself; it is widely regarded and appreciated for what it is—an emotional outlet, a political statement about the language and culture, and finally, simply entertainment.

Dot Miles, in her time, would have been a poet laureate of the Deaf community. Her poetic voice came out of a personal and communal anguish—how to resolve the conflicts from within and without. She wrote poetry intended to be lyrical and evocative, to elevate the view of the language as one worthy of literary regard, and as she tells us, she wrote out of a deep need to reach out to others. Her poetry was politically charged, but it was also about unrequited love and wistful memories of her childhood. Miles loved deeply and invested her creative energies heavily in her poetry. Today poetry and poets can afford to be irreverent, cheeky, and politically mischievous, but in 1975, Miles was very serious about her work. In a videotape, we see her refer to the original name, "the sign language" when referring to the language of her poetry, a reminder that at the time she began her experimentation, the idea of ASL as a name for the language was still new.

As Deaf people watched poets and storytellers perform on public stages, their view of the language was transformed. Sam Supalla's popular "Best Whiskey of the West" is borrowed in part from Ray and Charles Eames's 1977 film *Powers of 10*, and from cowboy stories popular in schools for the deaf (see Merv Garretson's "Cowboy Poem"). In *Powers of 10*, the camera moves from the smallest molecule out through the body to galaxies in outer space; in Sam's story a cowboy drinks a shot of whiskey that propels him through the roof, through the sky, past the clouds, and into outer space. The cowboy continues flying past the moon, Mars (with Martians waving), and through the Milky Way until he is caught in the hand of a Supreme Being. The Being takes one look at his watch, announces it is not the cowboy's time, and throws him back. Down he goes, again through the galaxies, the planets, into earth's atmosphere, and finally back seated on the bar stool. Supalla's meticulously planned choice of handshapes, movements together with management of the face, is only one part of the performance. What Deaf people recognize immediately is the mimicking of film and camcorder technique in Supalla's story: using hands and signs to depict close-ups as though there were a camera panning across a landscape. This is storytelling for a media-savvy generation, a pleasing blending of the two visual grammars into a single story.

Stretching tradition further, David Rivera and Manny Hernandez use *television* rather than film technique in stories about sports, incorporating slow motion and replay shots into their descriptive structures. In contrast to Sam Supalla, who insists on crisp signing technique, Rivera blurs his handshapes slightly and makes his movements wide, giving an urban, hip edge to his signing. Evon Black brings the history of Black deaf schools to the public stage in her one-woman shows about African-American Deaf culture, riffing on subjects ranging from hair combing in Black Deaf schools and mimicking signing styles of the older African-American deaf. Not only is there new technique and content in storytelling and poetry today, but there is also a revival of old styles, and the audience is pleased by the juxtaposition of the old and new.

The anxiety of culture is a problem of the times: when is a Deaf person "Deaf" or "deaf"? When or where is "culture"? Perhaps it is no longer useful to count how many or who, but instead to focus on the *cultural,* where meaning is made—for the moment and in the moment. The collective experience of Deaf people is not necessarily one that every Deaf person shares or even knows directly, but the residue of this history permeates the experience of Deaf people. The central role of deaf schools in their history remains today as each new generation of Deaf children and their parents makes decisions about schooling. The lingering and lasting effects of separation and segregation have created overlapping yet distinct cultures within the community. The struggle to use voice and manage voice and to make sign language intelligible underlies nearly every political act of the community. Voice as a technology continues to grow and change as Deaf people manage its use through history. Invention and innovation in performance have characterized sign poetry and storytelling from the first gathering of Deaf people during colonial times to this day. The *cultural* is neither here nor there, but is borne through history, made anew by the circumstances of the present. *Cultures* suggest a fixedness of place and time. The *cultural* offers a fluid idea of how experience and expression come together. The cultural resides in things, in behaviors as well as in performance.

George Veditz delivered his fiery speech in sign language and later wrote it in English. Dot Miles signed and wrote her poetry simultaneously, trying to find the point where the two languages meet. Clayton Valli worked with his hands, practicing the positioning of hand and movement until the line was perfectly crafted, then recorded on videotape and sold to ASL classrooms across the country. The *cultural* is never universal or without time, but exists in the moment of expression. The long history of the language is delivered to the performance, and in the performing, it is made anew. Veditz, Miles, and Valli used the same language and struggle for expression, but in each there is a fresh and new expression of language and idea, made real for the time they lived in.

7

The Promise of Culture

One of the authors, Tom Humphries, was introduced quite suddenly to the Deaf community in 1964 while he was working as a teenager at his uncle's furniture store. A vocational rehabilitation counselor had learned that a deaf worker was employed at the store, so he came to visit and explained that his job was to provide training, including financial support for a college education for deaf and handicapped high school students. He could help pay for Tom to go to a college in Washington, D.C., where the students were deaf like himself.

Tom had never heard of Gallaudet, but with few other options after high school, he decided to enroll. At the age of seventeen, he left his small hometown and traveled to Washington, D.C., to begin his college education. When he arrived, however, he was not prepared for the encounter. Though he was deaf, he found himself in an environment where he could understand very few people. He knew no sign language. He had grown up among hearing people and had almost no contact with Deaf people (though he had a distant cousin who was deaf, because she went to the school for the deaf and he did not, they did not know each other). What he noticed first was that the other students seemed to have a familiarity and an ease with each other that he did not have and at the time, could not imagine ever having. As he took his first walk around campus, he was struck and dismayed by how alienated he felt. He had no idea there was such a place as this.

In the days and weeks following, Tom reached some important conclusions. First, he realized that if he was to meet his basic social needs, he would have to change. He had grown up as a "hearing person who didn't hear," meaning that his experience in life had been as the only deaf person among a family and community of people who hear. Now he was in a different context where he was not "the only one." The accommodation he had received in his hometown because he was the only deaf person no longer served him in this new environment. While patience was shown him initially, his inability to sign or join in the activities of the group was quickly becoming a liability.

Second, he realized that he would have to learn the language and that it was not simply a matter of learning signs. By the end of his first week, he began to understand the enormity of the task. This was a complicated and different language from his native English. He could not simply match signs to English words he already knew. He had assumed before he came that he would learn the language quickly, but he was beginning to see that it was more sophisticated and nuanced than he realized. Each day was a struggle to use the language. His ability to speak and lipread English was not of much value here. Communication was rapid and complex, and he could not keep up.

The most daunting realization of all was that he was living among a group of people who shared a history he did not know and who in turn knew little about how he had grown up and lived as a deaf person. He had befriended a few whose experiences were similar to his, but he could not avoid daily contact and interaction with those who had been signing all their lives. Many of them had known each other before coming to college, often through sports because their schools for the deaf played against each other. Many seemed to know each others' families. He did not know that there was a social network of Deaf families and Deaf communities. He would later find out that some of his classmates' parents were Deaf and some had several Deaf relatives.

Their ways of doing things were strange to him. They seemed to move assertively in space in ways that he did not. Their movements seemed larger and more obvious, at times when he thought they should be smaller and less conspicuous. It was like he had moved to a foreign country where he, alone among them, had no clue how to behave. He could not figure out how to manage a signed conversation, where to look and what to say first. Despite his efforts, it seemed as if he was often looking at the wrong signer, or entirely missed what a signer was saying because he turned too late to look.

Worse, he had to admit he was feeling uncomfortable in this environment. He was surprised at his reaction at being in the company of other deaf people. In his hearing family and community, he had always been taught that he was special, that no other deaf person was like him, and that it was undesirable to be like other deaf people. He believed that he was an exception. His value of himself was tied to his belief that he had managed to transcend negative images of deaf people in society. His view of sign language was especially strong. He thought it was inadequate and of little use in an English-speaking world. Yet he soon realized that his view of himself contradicted those of the Deaf people around him.

He could see, to his astonishment, that they delighted, even celebrated, those things that made him uncomfortable. They were clearly at ease with their sign language. They valued individuals among themselves who were skilled, artistic, and creative with the language. They asserted pride in themselves as Deaf individuals and as a community. Not a day went by that Tom didn't sense their message to him that he had been brought to a world much more real and possible than the one from which he came. And, over time, without being aware of exactly the moment when or how it happened, he began to feel the same way. As he learned the language and the ways of life of the community, he came to believe that he was being rescued from a life where he had communicated with others on a very small scale.

As Tom's circle of friends expanded beyond the handful of people who came from backgrounds similar to his, he learned more about what it meant to be Deaf. It wasn't easy. He wasn't just learning about Deaf people; though he didn't know it then, he was in the process of becoming Deaf himself. Much like a person who moves to a different country and over the years feels less like a foreigner, he became more unable to distinguish himself from other students. A simple but telling moment occurred when he first called himself "Deaf" in sign. Until that moment, he had called himself "hard of hearing." He believed that it more correctly identified him as being someone who could speak, and who was different from people whom he had spent his life trying *not* to be. It was strange he should call himself hard of hearing because he had no ability to hear. He had lost all his hearing at the age of six from exposure to antibiotics. Now, he found himself including himself as one of those he used to think of as *them*. From learning about Deaf people, he had moved on to learn to be Deaf.

What changed was not immediately clear to him. He knew that he had developed a level of comfort as a signer and that he no longer felt so uncomfortable in his own skin. He felt included in a way that he hadn't felt back home among his hearing family and community. In fact, he began to feel quite angry at his own older attitudes and misguided ideas about Deaf people and ASL. He began to question where he had gotten those ideas and why. Of course, he knew that they had come from a lack of public awareness. He knew that people who hear had some strong misconceptions that made it difficult for them to see Deaf people as they saw themselves. In the minds of the people he grew up with, speech and language were the same thing and people who did not speak were not capable of development in any normal fashion. He knew that he once had believed learning could not progress very quickly or very far without speech. Abstract and scholarly thought was possible through spoken communication, not through gestures or signs.

He knew that in the minds of people who hear, redemption for Deaf people was through integration within the society of hearing people. Deaf people who choose to live together in communities and favor their sign language over learning how to be more like hearing people were considered unfortunate. It made them dependent and limited their potential. He knew that the public had other ideas about Deaf people as well: that they were naive, that they could not enjoy life without sound, that their world was small, and that they struggled to accomplish the normal routines of everyday life in a hearing world. Only by learning to speak, learning English, and, in general, learning to interact more successfully among hearing people could they overcome these limitations. But even if they successfully integrated, they would always lack a quality to their lives that could not be retrieved: they would never know the experience of sound.

These attitudes had never bothered him, or rather, he had never let himself be bothered by these attitudes before. But by the time he had graduated from college, he became angry about these ideas. There was a deep divide between the way Deaf people saw themselves and the way hearing people saw them. There was almost no place in public consciousness for his hard-earned realization that Deaf people led rich social lives; in fact, the public held strong misconceptions that guided their assumptions. While he was a college student, he had watched educators of the deaf object strenuously against the idea that a signed language could be a human language. It was common to hear comparisons between gesturing and sign language, with the conclusion that true languages involved speech. But people who hear and speak had determined these standards. Furthermore, they had designed and created institutions of knowledge, systems and practices under which Deaf people were raised. It was not surprising that so few Deaf people were allowed to rise to positions within such systems. If they could, they would design ways of living that Deaf people wanted for themselves, and introduce alternative ways of thinking about language and culture. Once the issues were reframed in these ways, Tom sensed among many Deaf people a growing realization of injustice.

Tom began to hear about studies of sign language and that a new name had recently been devised, "the American sign language." He was cautious about these new claims because they seemed to come from a community that had once passed negative judgment on sign language. But these claims felt different. Though at first he saw himself as uninformed, the studies' arguments had an undeniable appeal, and he watched as an undercurrent of debate and emotion began to circulate. On one side, many of his Deaf friends could not accept that sign language was equivalent to spoken language, believing instead that it was not a language but a gestural system that could be translated by matching signs to English words. On the other side, hearing people began to argue that these Deaf people were wrong, and that their denial of sign languages was misguided. Tom found himself surrounded by Deaf people who were deeply conflicted, and who were anxiously watching each other to see how the debate would play out. Who among their friends and colleagues would take which side of the debate? What were the stakes in these arguments? Would their jobs be affected by the debate? The entire Deaf community seemed to be as confused as he was.

As time passed, Tom became aware of a yearning, and sensed

that others did too, for a new way of talking and thinking about Deaf people. Older themes that embraced older ideas about Deaf people seemed inadequate, even patronizing, in the face of a new discourse that recognized history, language, and the notion of "culture."

If Deaf people were to be thought of as constituting a cultural group, how would one describe such a group? Cultures have traditions, customs, rituals, art, literature, modes of dress, and even cuisines; how would such a concept be translated to describing Deaf people? There would need to be evidence for Deaf culture. Some of the first attempts to write about Deaf culture described boundaries and membership because boundaries were beginning to blur and become porous.[1] These first attempts at writing asked: Who is Deaf? What is American Sign Language? Who uses it? In 1950, these questions would be answered as: Deaf people are those who attend schools for the deaf and go to Deaf clubs. American Sign Language must be what English is not. But in 1970, the questions weren't as easy to answer. Not all Deaf people graduated from schools for the deaf, and Deaf clubs were declining. The problem of membership was really a question of authenticity, or who can be called Deaf or what was real American Sign Language—a question that pitted Deaf and hearing people alike against each other.

When Tom arrived in this community, one of the first things he noticed was that his path into it was one of several. Like him, most Deaf people were born to hearing families. Within this group, there were several ways of finding the community: Some families had hearing parents who signed and encouraged their deaf children's association with other Deaf people, easing their acquisition of the language and knowledge of the community. Some were born into hearing families who intended to raise them without sign language, or "orally," as it was called. Their entry to the community came later in life, often when parents relinquished their control of their children. At some point, either by accident as in Tom's case, or by design or plan, Tom and other deaf people like himself met each other and began to share goals.

The other author, Carol Padden, was born into a Deaf family. Carol's parents are Deaf, as well as three of her four grandparents. Her older brother is also Deaf. Carol's parents were both faculty members at Gallaudet College, and raised both Carol and her brother bilingually in ASL and English. As a child growing up in the 1960s, the Deaf children and adults she knew attended schools for the deaf. Deaf clubs were places to frequent, and the social events of her family, from Deaf theater to picnics and visits at friends' houses, were often with other Deaf people. Not until her family's first telephone arrived in 1968 was it possible for her family to make a text telephone call to other friends in the community. Before the telephone, Carol's family would write letters to friends, or simply drop in to visit. Calls to hearing people needed the help of a friend such as a neighbor or coworker.

Despite not having a telephone until later, life in Carol's family was unremarkable in that she had not acquired a sense of being very different from her parents or their friends. Her conversations with almost everyone she met were in ASL and even when the topic of discussion turned to deaf and hearing people, there was a sense of her family sharing experiences with other families in the community. Being without hearing was part of the landscape in which Carol grew up, neither onerous nor unusually special.

Carol's family and community experiences provided her with ways of thinking about herself and her relationships with others. As a child, she knew about hearing people. They lived on her block, and her neighbor would make phone calls for her mother. They were coworkers in factories and print shops, also principals and superintendents of schools for the deaf. They were also colleagues of her parents at Gallaudet College. Most hearing people she saw in her neighborhood did not sign, but spoke English. Some hearing people whom her parents knew or worked with signed very well. She watched how her parents interacted with hearing people—her mother spoke to her hearing relatives and coworkers, and her father tended to write messages or use her mother to interpret. She grew to understand that her family and friends lived side by side with significant numbers of people who hear. Neighborhood children with whom she played were different than her parents and brother. She learned to communicate with them differently and to recognize who was and who was not Deaf.

As she began third grade, Carol's parents decided to transfer her from a school for the deaf and enroll her in a public school with hearing children who did not sign. Unlike her older brother, Carol was hard of hearing and had begun to wear hearing aids. Because she was learning to speak English, a school administrator suggested that her parents consider transferring her to a public school.

When she arrived for the first day of school, she was amazed at the size of her new school. At her old school for the deaf, her classes had few students, and she knew most of the adults in the school, but in her new school, her class had thirty students, all strangers to her. Her sign language was of little use to her. She had no interpreter; instead she was expected to use her newly developed English language skills. She had learned to speak English, to pronounce words and sentences, but she did not know how to use the English language. She had to struggle to figure out what her teacher and classmates meant by what they said. Faced with ways of using English that she had not learned in her family and community, she found herself in many unfamiliar contexts and situations.

As she left home each morning on the bus for school, she felt as if she was leaving the ease and comfort of her Deaf family for the strangeness and unpredictability of her school environment. The bus ride was a journey between worlds, each day deepening her sense of how different her family and community were to the rest of the world. Though she felt anxiety traveling to this new culture, she also found herself curious and attracted. At home, hearing people felt distant, but at school, she was in closer contact with them. These were people who lived in her neighborhood but whose lives were distant from her family. There was something exotic about them—their way of dress, their talk, their music, their social relationships. She wanted to learn what it all meant. It was one thing to see hearing people and their ways on TV, but quite another to spend her days among them, up close and personal. There was a seductiveness in their difference: how they used English and the ways that they thought, acted, and spoke.

Later, as she looked back on her earlier experiences, she was shocked to learn how small the world of her family and friends was compared to this world of hearing people. As she walked on the campuses of deaf schools and at Gallaudet College, where her parents taught, the buildings felt as if at the right scale, but at a hearing school, the halls seemed longer, the rooms oversized. At her former school she could talk with any child she chose, but at the new school, she needed to be more selective because she could not understand all of the children. There were many Deaf people in her world and her time spent with them was busy, full, and complex, but here was another world, larger, busier, and more complex than she had imagined.

Comfortable and confident among Deaf people, she became self-conscious and watchful in her new relationships. She was uncertain of how to handle the reaction of hearing people to the fact that she did not hear. Her hearing status became one of the most obvious and noticeable things about her in this new environment. She found herself dealing with a new perception of her, occasions of misunderstanding who she was and what her abilities were. Her social skills now needed to be adapted for use with hearing people.

The ways that hearing people seemed to think about Deaf people were strange to Carol. When she was growing up, she had often heard Deaf people's stories about hearing people, and now she was learning hearing people's stories about Deaf people. She knew that hearing people thought of Deaf people as handicapped and that they believed if they should ever become deaf themselves, their life as they knew it would end. But she was not prepared to see how their ideas became realized in their interaction with her. Hearing people found the fact of deafness, and by extension, deaf people, more strange and disastrous than she did. They said so in their words to her, and in their reactions to her family and friends.

While with hearing people, she was expected to adapt to their behaviors and to their ways of talking. She realized that their view of her as handicapped could not be overcome; it was too deeply rooted in their culture. When she spoke English, they noticed her "hard of hearing" accent and sometimes commented on it. If she brought friends home from school, she had to remember that her parents were foreign to her friends. If she wanted to bring her parents to school, her parents would be foreign there as well. A lot of her time and energy was consumed remembering herself as ordinary while being regarded as strange.

By the time Carol entered college, there was a growing interest in sign languages. With his colleagues, William Stokoe had published a dictionary of American Sign Language demonstrating that linguistic principles could be applied to the study of sign languages.[2] For Carol, linguistics offered a way to understand her experience of moving between two languages that were equivalent in expressive power, yet different in what they expressed. Telling a story in American Sign Language could include detail that would typically not be included in a similar story in English, yet both languages held equivalent possibilities. Instead of embracing these new ideas, she found her family and community in a state of alarm and confusion. Her parents were unsure whether their sign language should take on a new name. Her friends complained about the proliferation of new technical names for different types of signing, and said that the new ideas threatened to upset a comfortable way of existence.

The two authors represent two different pathways into the community. Most Deaf people come to the community not through family, but through contact with other Deaf people at school. Carol's experience of childhood in a Deaf family is comparatively rare. Yet these pathways become implicated in how labels like Deaf and hearing are used. Carol's family is Deaf. Tom grew up in a hearing environment. Tom's status depended on his ability to pass as someone who knows ASL well. Some days he seemed to pass well, and other days, someone would ask a direct question, "Are you Deaf or hearing?" in order to understand his background. The question came less often as he became more adept at "being" Deaf.

Questions of authenticity were important in the early years of talking about "Deaf culture," in the sense that there needed to be "criteria" for the new vocabulary. Who were those called "us" and those called "others"? Where did Deaf culture begin and other cultures end? Was Deaf culture a subculture or an entirely separate culture? These were questions that came from having to define being Deaf by a set of criteria that Deaf people had never used before. Deaf people had long been defined according to hearing ability and the age when they became deaf, whether at birth or later. Now, the criteria became skill in ASL, ability to carry oneself as though appearing Deaf, and family background. Which of these experiences count the most? Suddenly, there was a problem of definition and how to assess different pathways of experience.

By the time the word "culture" began to be associated with Deaf people, their lives had already changed. In the latter part of the twentieth century, economic shifts leading to changes in the types of work Deaf people did influenced changes in their social practices and beliefs. Deaf people were not alone in experiencing this trans-formation; similar alterations have taken place in other ethnic and cultural groups as well.[3] The transformation moved Deaf people into new spheres, onto public stages as well as into different types of work. They would need new language and new practices for the new places where they found themselves. The word "culture" pro-vided a word, a new tool and device for describing and under-standing Deaf people and their new lives.

The way that Deaf people see themselves and their explanation of themselves is historically grounded. Deaf people in the United States are descendants of a long lineage extending back into the eighteenth century with roots in the first schools for the deaf in Europe. When Tom lived alone among hearing people, he knew little of other deaf people, and was unaware of any history of Deaf people. He thought of himself as unique and alone. When he met Deaf people for the first time and observed an unusual familiarity among them, it would take him a long time to understand that this was a product of a history together and an even longer history ex-tending before them. While Carol saw herself living as part of a community of Deaf people, she realized later that she had inher-ited beliefs and ways of thinking that had been passed down by previous generations of Deaf people. She was a present link in a stream of collective acts and thoughts extending over generations.

The task of Deaf people approaching the end of the twentieth century has been the projection of this history into public space. As we explained in Chapter 5, the National Theatre of the Deaf was an early experiment of Deaf actors presenting new knowledge about their language and culture on a public stage. In this public voice, Deaf people explained themselves in terms of a complete wellness, whole bodies and whole lives. They also used humor and allegory to challenge an older way of thinking about themselves. Being Deaf was not a consequence of not hearing. Being Deaf was an ex-istential experience, complete in itself and not a consequence of broken bodies but the outcome of biological destiny. As many Deaf people came to say "I don't want to be hearing," they shocked even themselves and their hearing public, but the experiment in self-description resonated strongly among Deaf people.

The recognition of sign language, not by linguists or scholars, but by Deaf people themselves, was a pivotal moment. While Deaf people had been aware that their sign language met their needs and provided them with an aesthetic pleasure that only languages can provide, the realization that sign languages were equal to yet uniquely interesting among human languages brought to Deaf people a sense of vindication and pride. To possess a language that is not quite like other languages, yet equal to them, is a powerful realization for a group of people who have long felt their language disrespected and beseiged by others' attempts to eliminate it.

Before sign language became so public, the language bonded the group together and kept alive rich channels of cultural circulation. Its unusual qualities kept away outsiders because Deaf people believed there was little interest in the language outside the group. They had been told by others that their language wasn't worth preserving. Yet part of their private use of sign language came from a desire to protect their private world, to have something that would insulate them from those who might do them emotional or physical harm. Coming to accept that ASL was an object of public interest and that it should be taught to others was a difficult transition.

As ASL moved into a public space, it quickly became clear that hearing people wanted to study it and describe how it works. What had been private and closely held by Deaf people was now being talked about and written in positive ways, but also in ways that Deaf people themselves hardly recognized. They were unused to seeing their language discussed in the jargon of scientists. They had their own "folk" theories about ASL. They often talked about it as having an "art" to it or a "preferred mode of expression," and it was difficult for many to relate to the new discourse about it, the discourse of "phonology," "morphology," and other linguistic terminology.

Just as surprising was the increasing demand of hearing people to learn the language. Before 1960, few hearing people were ASL signers. If they learned the language, they did so from an association with Deaf people such as working at a school for the deaf, or from a Deaf relative. A very small number studied the language and learned it in a class. But by the 1970s, there had been a sharp increase in demand for ASL instruction, a development for which the community was not prepared. The way sign language had been taught in the past was as a translation of English words. Teachers would give students a list of English vocabulary or phrases and then for each, give a matched translation in signs. What was taught was how to translate English into signs.

Slowly, as more knowledge was gained about the structure of ASL, the teaching of ASL became more like foreign-language teaching. The demand for ASL classes created two problems. The first was pedagogical: How do you teach a sign language? Many who had skill in the language did not know how to explain it. They had grown up learning English grammar, but had never been taught ASL grammar. The problem became: Which form of the language was "real"? Which form of the language was borrowed from English? Which form of the language was coincidentally similar to English, but not English? There would be heated debates about ASL—in ASL.

The second problem for Deaf people was to overcome their anxieties, both personal and collective, about the fate of their language as it became increasingly more public. In the early 1970s, Deaf people were unsure of the motives of hearing linguists—were they truly interested in describing their language, or had they other goals? Furthermore, what were Deaf people to make of the growing interest in learning ASL as a foreign language? How did hearing people plan to use their knowledge of the language? Would they learn the language in order to communicate with Deaf people, or to dominate them? Only after a decade of rapid growth without dire consequences did the community relax and begin to see the advantage of the proliferation of ASL in foreign-language teaching.

Besides the problems of agreeing who was Deaf and the problem of their language becoming public, embracing "culture" as a means of public identity meant agreeing on what to call themselves. The 1960s and 1970s saw a movement to replace the English term "deaf" with "hearing impaired." Deaf people had always used a sign, transcribed as DEAF, which referred to themselves. The sign had been translated into English as "deaf," but it is an inaccurate translation. The English word refers to loss of hearing, but the ASL sign refers to a difficult to translate quality, the essence of what DEAF people are. The sign would be more accurately translated as "we" or "us" (DEAF people), and carries the meaning of hearing loss only secondarily. Deaf people are deaf, but not solely this characteristic.

Despite the lack of precise translation, Deaf people wanted to retain the English word "deaf" as the appropriate translation for the sign instead of "hearing impaired." The problem with "hearing impaired" is first that it has no historical basis in the language, that is, Deaf people refer to themselves as not hearing, and not that they have an impairment in hearing. Second, it refers to those who do not hear, but are not ASL signers, as Tom once was. "Hearing impaired" includes people who do not want to be considered signers and are not Deaf. By contrast, DEAF refers to people who are completely without hearing, and to people who can hear some and call themselves "hard of hearing."

Deaf people knew that their community included those with varying degrees of hearing. This was confusing to Tom when he met Deaf people for the first time. He had assumed before he arrived at Gallaudet that Deaf people were totally and profoundly without hearing. He later realized that some of the people he considered most Deaf actually could hear quite well, even well enough to use the telephone. He was surprised, more than once, to see Deaf people he knew using their hearing in various ways. For example, one of the first things that he noticed upon moving into the dormitory was that on a regular basis his dorm mates would gather around the TV in the lounge and watch a program interpreted by a Deaf student who could hear enough to understand the TV. Tom would meet Deaf people from Deaf families who called themselves Deaf, but could hear better than he could. Ironically, he was still calling himself "hard of hearing."

Deaf people encompass a diverse group of people, unified by the experience of living among Deaf people and ASL. Hearing level plays a different role in the community. Carol grew up knowing she was Deaf. But on numerous occasions, she had to explain that she was "hard of hearing" to those curious about her hearing level.

To the world of the hearing, signers, nonsigners, people recently deafened, and people who were hard of hearing share the quality of hearing impairment, but in fact, each group has little in common with each other, other than a physical characteristic of not hearing. Becoming a signer is a process of socialization in the same way it is a process of socialization to become a deaf nonsigner. The culture is defined not solely by degree of not hearing, though the fact of not hearing is a large part of how Deaf people interact with one another. Tom, without a trace of auditory response on his audiogram, was not Deaf until he learned to be. Carol, with more hearing evident on her audiogram, was hard of hearing as well as Deaf from birth.

The idea of culture offers the possibility of separation and inclusion at the same time. Culture provides a frame for Deaf people to separate themselves from an undefined group of those with hearing impairments, but at the same time, they are included in the world of human communities that share long histories, durable languages, and common social practices. Separation allows Deaf people to define political goals that may be distinct from other groups. Inclusion allows Deaf people to work toward humanist goals that are common to other groups such as civil rights and access. In this way, the idea of culture is not merely an academic abstraction, but very much a "lived" concept. Tom remembers his early encounter with the idea that there was a culture of Deaf people, in fact many different Deaf cultures around the world. It implied a connectivity to others that was intoxicating to a young man whose life was once based on having a "special" place in a world of people who hear. The attraction of the ordinary, the sameness, the sharedness, and the sense of roots in the past that it offered was strong.

For us and others in the Deaf community, culture also offers a way to counter world views too heavily influenced by others. Deaf people have long lived under the benevolence and care of others whose plans and aspirations often isolated Deaf people from each other and labeled them in ways that left them uneducated and alone. Culture offers the possibility of making Deaf people whole. It assumes lines of transmission of ways of being from generations past, as long ago as hundreds of years. Culture provides a way for Deaf people to reimagine themselves as not so much adapting to the present, but inheriting the past. It allows them to think of themselves not as unfinished hearing people but as cultural and linguistic beings in a collective world with one another. It gives them a reason for existing with others in the modern world.

More attractive than any other promise that the idea of culture holds for Deaf people is the thread of connection to the past. The fear of banishment and elimination has dogged Deaf people throughout most of their history. George Veditz worried about the future of the sign language in 1913, and today Deaf people continue to worry. In 1913, Veditz railed against hearing people who would prohibit the use of sign language and develop methods of education that would isolate deaf children from sign language. Today, the same concerns exist; there are doctors and teachers who say that they are ambivalent about the future of sign language while they are enthusiastic about the future of technology like cochlear implants.

The medical community's narrow focus on deaf people as patients to be alleviated of their affliction has always been a source of anxiety within the community. The idea of "culture" outlines the terms of a counterargument. It demands considerations of equal treatment, justice, and political voice for a group of people who find themselves in a highly politicized environment such as medicine and disability.

A generation of young Deaf people have grown to adulthood with a vocabulary of culture and language that is only thirty years old. Where once the words "Deaf culture" and "American Sign Language" were controversial, they have since eased into everyday talk, and are used now as unselfconsciously as "the sign language" once was. Now "Deaf culture" has taken on a new layer of meaning: it has become a code for challenging the ideologies of others who have a stake in deaf children and deaf adults. The ideology of those who believe deaf children should grow up without sign language conflicts with Deaf culture. As the medical profession continues to hold that doctors have privileged expertise on deafness, Deaf culture has come to represent an alternative view of humans under their care, calling into question their goals of medical treatments and rehabilitation.

An ironic lesson to be taken from the short history of "culture" in Deaf people's history is how a concept long used for *hearing* people around the world can be so eagerly adapted for use by Deaf people. The long history of scholars writing about spoken language grammars has come to be enormously useful for describing sign languages as well. Perhaps this is the true lesson of human cultures and languages, that our common human nature is found not in how we are alike, but in how we are different, and how we have adapted to our differences in very human ways.

8

Cultures into the Future

As we begin the twenty-first century, large issues loom ahead. In April 2003, the National Institutes of Health announced that the sequencing of the human genome had been completed, enabling the identification of almost 30,000 genes that make up the human being, including those involved in genetic deafness. A few months later, the Modern Language Association announced a significant increase in the number of colleges and universities now offering classes in American Sign Language, placing it among the fifteen most commonly taught languages across the country.[1]

Doctors and scientists are approaching a time when they will be able to identify and "correct" genetic deafness, which may lead to the elimination of deaf communities and sign languages. Yet sign languages are generating more public attention and interest than at any other time in their history. How can two conflicting impulses exist at the same time—to eradicate deafness and yet to celebrate its most illustrious consequence, the creation and maintenance of a unique form of human language?

This conflict of impulses, to "repair" on the one hand, and to acknowledge diversity on the other, must be one of the deepest contradictions of the twenty-first century. Deaf people, whether they like it or not, live their lives in the middle of this contradiction. They share their predicament with disabled and ethnic groups including, for example, Jewish communities and Icelandic people, who also worry about what the Human Genome Project has in store for them.

Each chapter in this book has introduced themes that have resonated time and again throughout the history of Deaf people in America, and they continue to resonate today, in the age of the microchip and the gene. These are themes of silence and the problem of voice, of dominance and control in institutions, and of the struggle to shape the future of deaf children and adults.

The first schools for the deaf in the early eighteenth century were built during a groundswell of optimism in the power of institutions to change the lives of the poor and afflicted, including deaf children. By the end of the nineteenth century, there were more than eighty-seven such schools established throughout the United States.[2] Once deaf children had been brought within these institutions, the relationship between caretaker and deaf child became fraught with issues of power and control. Only six months after the Pennsylvania Institution for the Deaf and Dumb was founded in 1820, there was a scandal and their principal was accused of improper contact with female bodies. If the female students had tried to speak out about what was done to them, they were made silent. They had only the matron to interpret their accounts to the caretakers. They could not speak directly to those who were responsible for their care because the members of the board of directors of the school could not understand their sign language.

Deaf leaders at the beginning of the twentieth century turned to film as a way to confront the problem of voice. Using this new technology, their sign language could be projected visibly onto a screen for audiences around the country. The language was to become both a vehicle for communication and a conduit for their ideas. But there was still the problem of being understood in sign language. Even if they could project their language onto a screen, would their signs be understood? To communicate their message to those who did not know the language, the films were accompanied by scripts that could be read by a hearing person during the screening. The struggle for voice was both a problem of translation and a problem of mode, from sign to speech.

By the middle of the twentieth century, Deaf people had built a broad network of clubs, associations, and literary societies throughout the country, but these were spaces largely kept out of public view. As the new National Theatre of the Deaf recruited actors from clubhouses and schools around the country, the struggle for voice moved onto the public stage. In 1967, Deaf actors began to speak to hearing audiences about the life they had led before joining the NTD. In *My Third Eye,* an original production developed from a theater workshop, Deaf actors compiled skits that ranged from the achingly personal to the lightheartedly comedic, from a dark allegory hinting at inhumane treatment in schools to an uplifting choreography of hands in a sign language song. With hearing actors who spoke on the same stage while Deaf actors signed their lines, the stories that Deaf actors told were about private lives, now brought into full view for a receptive public. Their voice was now audible, but how would they describe their experiences in ways that would make them intelligible? Linguists offered a new vocabulary for sign language and its different layers of meaning. Deaf culture was likewise added to a quickly expanding list of new words and phrases, satisfying a demand to explain Deaf people's lives in ways that compared them to communities around the world.

The rapid expansion of voice technologies—from sign language interpreters to text pagers and video telephone relays—has made the problem of voice less a problem of access. Deaf people can draw from many technologies to render their sign language intelligible to others, from the speaking lectern, over the telephone lines, in classroom lecture halls, and in nearly any public space they choose. Deaf people now have a remarkable capacity to translate their sign language into spoken form, more than any other time in their history.

Yet Deaf people today face the most important challenge of voice: How do they voice their concerns at a time when medical technologies and genetic engineering have stated their goal as the elimination of deafness? Deaf people have been invited to participate in the ethical discussions around the Human Genome Project, but how can they make themselves intelligible among doctors and scientists cloaked with far more authority and power? How is it possible to communicate why there should be Deaf people and sign language in the future?

Each year thousands of deaf children are surgically implanted with electronic devices that direct electrical impulses to the cochlea to stimulate hearing. It is an intervention similar to hearing aids, designed to overcome a limitation in the ability to hear, but unlike hearing aids, it involves a technology that is surgically implanted into the cochlea. After surgery, the child begins a long course of rehabilitation that tailors the electronic device to the capabilities of the child, and then the child is trained to recognize sounds transmitted by the device. The child interacts first with the surgeon, then the specialists who train the child for the device. The child's teachers may also be enlisted in the task, to coordinate training with education.[3]

In the early years of the cochlear implant technology, some Deaf people spoke out, raising questions about the immediate and long-term effects of the devices, especially for young deaf children. A position paper written in 1985 on behalf of a Deaf organization asked questions about the medical risks of the procedure: the possibility of infection, and other hazards related to surgery such as facial paralysis, or if in the event of failure or technical obsolence of the device, the child would need to be reimplanted.[4] This attempt at voice had limited effect and was roundly dismissed by supporters of cochlear implant surgery as exaggerating the risks of the medical procedure and obstructing the desires of parents of deaf children and deaf individuals who wanted the devices. Harlan Lane, an eloquent hearing speaker and scientist, wrote several articles questioning the goals and the claims of cochlear implant specialists, but he was severely criticized by parents of deaf children with implants as being romantic about deafness and alarmist about the dangers of the surgery.[5]

In a recent book about cochlear implants, John Christiansen and Irene Leigh describe the early objections to cochlear implants as ranging from concerns about medical aspects to accusations of cultural genocide by doctors. Not surprisingly, claims of genocide were the most likely to draw fervent and violent opposition. Parents demanded to know why "militants" from "the deaf community" had the right to tell them what to do with their deaf children.[6] The problem of voice for Deaf people is that once they venture into cultural accounts, the landscape becomes difficult and unforgiving. In the clash of voices that resulted from these encounters, what became exposed were naive beliefs about the positions of the two sides, leading to deep insults and causing a wide breach that still exists today.

An Oscar-nominated documentary, *Sound and Fury,* brought home the intensity of emotion that surrounds parents who make decisions for or against a cochlear implant. The film followed several months in the life of a family with two adult sons, one hearing and one deaf, who became badly divided by the hearing son's decision to implant his deaf child despite the objections of his deaf brother, who also has a deaf child. As the camera shifted its eye between the hearing members of the family and the deaf members, the split between them was painfully obvious. The hearing son talked of his sadness and grief over having a deaf child, and the deaf son was clearly offended by his brother's decision to proceed with an implant for his nephew, believing the decision to be an implicit rejection of him and his sign language.[7]

Christiansen and Leigh describe the current environment in the "deaf community" as having reached a more tempered and balanced view of the devices because more Deaf adults have sought out this technology for themselves. Many Deaf people had hearing earlier in their lives, and wanted the device in order to restore their experience of hearing. When Deaf people describe why they have cochlear implants, they explain that they wish to reacquire the ability to hear, or to avail themselves of a tool in order to be able to speak English and interact with hearing speakers of English. They also reassure their friends that they have no intention of abandoning sign language, or changing with whom they are friends; instead they compare the device to hearing aids, which are tools for situations where additional hearing can improve interaction in spoken language.[8] Deaf people can believe that there is no incompatibility between cochlear implants and using sign language, but this view is not universally held in the field of cochlear implant surgery. There remains a conflict of goals, and still a problem of voice.

What is alarming about the rise in cochlear implant surgery are the kinds of social programs that are being developed after the surgery is performed to train deaf children to use the device. Some of these programs are eerily reminiscent of the "oralist" programs that were put into place at the turn of the twentieth century in schools for the deaf, where schools prohibited use of sign language in the classroom. Parents can request that their children be placed in classrooms where no sign language will be used in order that their children receive the full benefit of the cochlear implant, that is, constant exposure to speech. Some parents will say they support separating their implanted children not because they are against sign language, but because they are against its use in the early years of language development when the child most needs exposure to speech.

How do Deaf people communicate the risks of such social programs? Here, their voice begins to fail them because it refers to their language, history, and culture. There is a risk to delaying early exposure to a sign language just as there is a risk to delaying early exposure to speech for children who hear. Children who learn any language late in life run the risk of suffering the effects of language delay, which can include problems not only in using language, but also in performing other cognitive tasks.[9] If a deaf child succeeds with a cochlear implant, then the assumption is that the child will acquire spoken language normally. But if the child struggles with an implant for whatever reason, and there are children who do not do well with the device, then the possibility of language delay in either speech or sign language is significantly increased in environments where sign language is not allowed.

Linguistic risks aside, the problem of voice is how to speak out against an environment that believes separation of deaf children from a Deaf environment and culture is sound educational policy. If it is inhumane to prohibit Spanish-speaking children from using Spanish with their parents and friends so that they can learn English, why is it not also inhumane to prohibit deaf children from using sign language? Why is bilingualism considered normal in hearing children, even desirable, but not in deaf children? The answers to these two questions must be that deaf children require certain extreme conditions in order to learn, which places them in a class of children to be treated differently than other children. Describing deaf children as a special, unusual class of children even today is no different from the early years of the nineteenth century when deaf children were described as needing to be educated separately and were placed in institutions.

Surely educational programs can be developed that teach implanted children both speech and sign language. Surely the talents of doctors and scientists could be directed toward developing social programs that present speech and sign simultaneously to deaf children so that the benefits of bilingual acquisition in two modalities can be passed on to each new generation of deaf children. Instead the trend is a dangerously regressive one, threatening to return to the oralist project of the late nineteenth century.

On a different front, the Human Genome Project has brought another type of scrutiny to deaf people's bodies, and yet another challenge to the problem of voice. The genetic composition of the deaf person has been elevated to a new level of significance in recent years, coloring the dialogue with others, including doctors and geneticists. What are the goals of geneticists? What voice will be given to Deaf people as the Human Genome Project moves forward?

Geneticists have estimated that approximately half of the cases of deafness at birth or in early childhood can be traced to genetic causes, with the remaining caused by illness such as meningitis or other acquired causes.[10] The findings of geneticists about the proportion of deaf children in the two categories, genetic and nongenetic, may be new, but the observation is based on a very old classification of deaf children, dating back to the earliest days of deaf education in the United States. When the Pennsylvania Institution for the Deaf and Dumb opened in 1820, parents or guardians who were petitioning to place their children at the school were asked to identify whether their child "Was born deaf, or did . . . lose hearing through disease, and at what age?" In the case of John Carlin, admitted at the age of eight shortly after the school opened, it was noted in the admission book that he was "born deaf." Sarah Ann Ankins, admitted at age twelve, had a different notation: "lost hearing by poison-laurel at about 2 years old."

The transmission of deafness within families was noticed by American deaf schools very early in their history. John Carlin's admission form also noted that he had a "D&D [deaf and dumb] brother, Andrew," as did Elizabeth Williams, accepted as a student in 1821, who "has a D&D brother, Edward." The parents of Catherine and Mary Hartman, two deaf sisters admitted to the school, were listed as "both born deaf." Interestingly, hearing siblings of deaf family members were sometimes admitted to the school, probably because they were skilled users of sign language and behaved as did their deaf siblings. Anna Jarrat's record explains that "She is not and never was really deaf & dumb," though she "has a brother & sister deaf also . . . four sisters who hear . . . One of the sisters has three deaf & dumb children." Evidently the school did not have to remove Anna Jarrat on account of mistaken identification of deafness because the last note in her record says simply that she "Ran away from the Instn [institution]."

A century later, in 1900, the South Carolina Institution for the Deaf, Dumb and the Blind kept the same classification, and asked parents and guardians to list the cause of deafness on admission forms. Answers about causes of deafness ranged from "unknown" or "borned so," to those that listed specific causes: "beated head," "adenoids," "convulsions," and "catarrh," or inflammation of the mucous membranes. By this time, doctors, not parents, typically made the determination of the cause of deafness, and their diagnosis was reported on the form. The common and sometimes deadly childhood diseases were listed: measles, mumps, influenza, whooping cough, and meningitis, all of which can be accompanied by high fevers with subsequent damage to the inner ear, causing deafness. Parents also listed other ailments we now know are unlikely to cause deafness such as tonsils and adenoids. Until about 1960, the presence of swollen tonsils or adenoids was believed to cause deafness; as a consequence, many deaf children had their tonsils and adenoids removed in hopes their hearing would be restored. Simple colds or inflammation of membranes were often reported as a cause but most likely did not cause deafness. The child most likely became deaf by some other cause, or was born deaf but the deafness was not noticed until the presence of illness drew attention to it.

Petitioners were also asked to report "Any like affliction, say deafness or blindness, in the connection previous" and then whether the parents of the deaf child "were related before marriage." Annie Arrowood, born in 1895 in the county of Laurens, South Carolina, was duly recorded as having one brother who is also deaf but her parents are not related. Willie Fant's parents from Townville, however, were second cousins, and "her fathers grandmother was deaf."

Deaf people also draw on the same distinction between genetic and nongenetic causes when describing themselves, but they derive different meanings from those categories. Instead of drawing solely on medical attributes, the descriptions also note other characteristics. In the *Silent Worker,* a popular Deaf magazine from the 1950s, deafness was defined using descriptors common at the time. In an article about Frank T. Webb, for example, the writer describes how he moved up through the ranks to become a top machinist with the Modern Tooling Corporation in Los Angeles, explaining that he "was born in Guthrie Center, Iowa, the only deaf child in a family of four children."[11] In a later issue, Constantine Stanley Muslovski is described in an article as an enterprising barber who opened his own shop in Midland, Pennsylvania. As for the cause of deafness: "When Stan was just 18 months old, he was pedaling a tricycle across the street directly in front of his home. A truck under poor control struck little Stan and threw him off. His head struck the curb . . . The accident resulted in a serious brain concussion. It left Stan almost totally deaf."[12] Sidalise Hebert was a proprietor of her own beauty shop in Rayne, Louisiana, and "was in full possession of her faculties until twenty-six months of age, when multiple colds made her deaf."[13]

The descriptions are heavy with cultural subtext. We learn that Frank T. Webb "was born . . . the only deaf child in a family of four children," which indicates he is most likely deaf from birth. Because he did not hear at birth, he probably does not use speech. Furthermore, he has no Deaf relatives, otherwise it would have been mentioned. Stan Muslovski lost his hearing, as did Sidalise Hebert. After his accident, Muslovski retained some hearing, which most likely accounts for why he can speak English when communicating with customers in his barber shop. In 1953, when sign language interpreters had not yet arrived in the workplace, the articles explain how Deaf men and women managed their linguistic resources when working with hearing customers or hearing coworkers.

Some descriptions of a person's deafness seem quaint. Edwin Meade Hazel is described as a "mechanical wizard" who began his career as a keyboard operator at the University of Chicago Press, and later was promoted to the head of the casting department. He became deaf when at "two months old, a nurse applied the wrong solution for the alleviation of an earache, thereby seriously impairing his hearing."[14] Because hearing loss can go undetected for as long as the first year of an infant's life, it is just as likely that Hazel was born with the condition, and the incident with the nurse, if in fact it happened, had nothing to do with the hearing loss.

The drama of hearing loss after birth has emotional value; it often is told in the context of how this individual then attended a school for the deaf and later entered the Deaf community. It stands in contrast to other categories of deafness such as being born deaf or inheriting deafness from one's relatives. In 1953 genetic deafness was described in terms of how well-known the family was to the community. A Deaf daughter is described thus: "The youngest of the famed Watson family, Babette Krayeski, first saw the light of day in old Mexico, where her deaf father was running a store. In fact, all in the family but one were deaf."[15] Deaf children of Deaf parents are mentioned in nearly every issue of the *Silent Worker*, usually in the context of the relationship of the child and the family to the community.

As they appear in the pages of the *Silent Worker*, the personal narratives of Babette Krayeski, Frank T. Webb, Stan Muslovski, Sidalese Hebert, and Edwin Meade Hazel are partly about deafness, and partly about cultural categories. Each type of category is laden with meaning, and Deaf people tell stories about the categories in different ways. These details are reproduced in this popular Deaf magazine because Deaf readers have come to expect them; indeed much of their lives has involved talking about deafness using those types of categories.

As early as the middle of the nineteenth century, the fact that there were deaf children with deaf relatives drew the attention of scientists concerned with transmission of traits across generations. A figure no less illustrious than Alexander Graham Bell took up the cause of addressing the problem in a *Memoir upon the Formation of a Deaf Variety of the Human Race*. Expressing concern that there was "a tendency among deaf-mutes to select deaf-mutes as their partners in marriage," Bell argued that this tendency had in fact increased in the nineteenth century due to improved education, specifically the spread of schools for the deaf throughout the country, which by their very nature of congregating Deaf people had led to another undesirable outcome, the use of sign language among Deaf people. Arguing that the "propagation" of deafness by Deaf people was undesirable, indeed "a calamity to the world," Bell proposed social remedies: eliminating separate schools for the deaf, disallowing the use of sign language among Deaf children, and discouraging Deaf people from becoming teachers of deaf children.[16]

Yet Bell is described by the historian Brian Greenwald as a "positive eugenicist" because he did not advocate the outright prohibition of marriage between deaf people; instead Bell supported social measures such as integrated schooling and social diffusion of Deaf people so they would be less likely to seek out one another as either communicative or marriage partners. Bell's "softer" approach to genetic deafness stands in contrast to harsher proposals offered by "negative eugenicists" of his time such as Charles Davenport, who assiduously worked to enact laws requiring the sterilization of "feeble-minded" individuals to prevent them from reproducing further. Greenwald argues that Bell's personal familiarity with Deaf people and the community—both his mother and his wife were deaf—tempered his stance toward genetic deafness, and that he was able to distract more negative eugenicists from carrying out their ambitions for Deaf people as extensively as they did for the feeble-minded.[17]

Whatever his intentions, at the very least Alexander Graham Bell's *Memoir* and his dialogues with other eugenicists about genetic deafness set the stage for a discussion about deafness and its transmission across generations that continues virtually unchanged to this day. The Human Genome Project transforms that debate somewhat because there is new vocabulary about genes and the mechanisms of genetic transmission of deafness. Indeed it can be argued that even as more is known about genetic mechanisms, the social, cultural, moral, and ethical outlines of the debate remain difficult and highly charged.

Writing about the treatment of the disabled in the history of eugenics, Sharon Snyder and David Mitchell argue that it is misleading to characterize nineteenth-century eugenics as "bad science" or "quackery." They write: "While we have an investment in convincing ourselves that modern scientific methods continue to improve and grow increasingly more complex—and thus, accurate, Eugenic science was one of the most rigorous of its time."[18] Many of the classification tools and measures we use today for determining the presence of a condition are little changed from the eugenics period. The classification of deaf people into three categories—born deaf and cause unknown, deaf by illness, and deaf by genetic transmission—for example, is as durable today as it was when first used in schools for the deaf in the early nineteenth century. It can be found in any textbook on deaf education, and the categories are listed on demographic surveys of deaf children in school systems across the country. When deaf people are introduced to the public, their personal biographies often include reference to how they became deaf. Still today, just as in 1953 when the *Silent Worker* explained that Stan Musklovski lost his hearing at the age of eighteen months, these personal biographies of deafness position deaf people in the social sphere.

In 1908, Charles Davenport praised Alexander Graham Bell's reputation as a scientist, and asked if he would agree to serve on a committee on eugenics under the auspices of the American Breeders Association, which had as its goal, among others, to determine the "precise law of mating ensuring normal offspring from a parent with hereditary tendency towards ear defect." Today deaf parents are referred to genetics counselors in order to determine whether they may have deaf children. Though deaf people are said to have the right to make their own decisions about whether to bear deaf children, there is always the threat of "social responsibility." Deaf people should seek genetics counseling not because it is desirable to have information, but because the information will help them to "make their own decision" about having deaf children. One can ask: how does one make such a "decision" about the human value of having deaf children? What moral and ethical frame guides decisions such as these? Snyder and Mitchell insist that any program that wishes to examine the moral and ethical frameworks of genetics research and genetics information must acknowledge the long reach of the eugenics program, which holds its tight grip into the present, and will continue to do so into the future. In other words, we are not "free" to make our own decisions because our decisions are fraught with complications from our histories.

* * *

How do we resolve this conflict of voices, of Deaf people's ideas about deafness and sign language on the one hand, and doctors', scientists', and geneticists' ideas about the goals of medical technology and genetics on the other? The first step is recognizing the historical basis of this conflict—how these voices unfold in the way that they do.

Cochlear implant programs in hospitals and clinics typically require rehabilitation after surgery to realize the full benefit of an implant device, but programs vary in how they design this rehabilitation. Among deaf adults, there is little intervention in the language practices they already use, but programs are often much more directive with deaf children and their parents. Some clinics will claim on their websites that they encourage parents to use sign language after their children have had cochlear implants, but other programs are clearly less than enthusiastic. For those implementing such programs, sign language is seen as detracting from or hampering the development of speech and spoken language. Some programs will communicate in subtle ways that whether a child derives full benefit from the cochlear implant will depend on how well parents and caretakers commit fully to the program of rehabilitation, including shielding their children from sign language. Those who "weaken" will find their children possibly failing at the program.

This is an all-too-familiar refrain to Deaf people, one that seems inherent to the medical profession and its commitment to treating deafness as a disorder. What is different about this latest prohibition against sign language, however, is that it is coupled with a greater level of appropriation of deaf people's bodies: a surgical intervention. An object of technology is left in the body, as though to signal that after surgery, the deaf child is no longer the same and thus must be treated differently. The rehabilitation is the beginning of a new course of action, one that excludes signing. The intervention is reminiscent of the kinds of sinister forces against sign language that existed early in the twentieth century. How can a device, a small one at that, justify doctors' denial of all that Deaf people hold to be essential to their well-being?

Why is it so difficult for science to see a practical link between the cultural practices of Deaf people and the implant technology? Why is it easier for doctors to embrace speech and discourage signing? The answer must lie in the divergent histories of science and of Deaf people. Deaf people have not themselves been scientists, at least not in the same fields where their lives are likely to be influenced—medicine, genetics, or medical technology. They have been the recipients of this history, not participants in it. They have not been able to shape the goals of medical science. Deaf people's voices sound dissonant and harsh because they use a vocabulary unfamiliar to medical science, and they speak of ideas that ring hollow to scientists.

As more people have been implanted with cochlear devices, and as young deaf children with implants grow up to become adults, there will be more narratives about the benefits of the technology. We know now that individual children and adults experience widely varying levels of "hearing" after implantation. Some report hearing and understanding speech very well, and credit the technology with allowing them to communicate more easily in spoken language, as do people who find hearing aids useful. There are also adolescents and adults who describe other unpleasant sensations with the implants, causing some to abandon the implants after finding them not beneficial or useful.[19] Will these new narratives lead to a different view of the technology? Quite possibly not, because of the powerful mystique of technology; it is always "improving" and "changing." Deaf adults who abandon cochlear implants they received as children may be discredited because they were implanted with an older and less effective device, or because they have since become "culturally" influenced by other views.

Improved and better technology is not likely to be a way out of moral and cultural quandaries; we will still need humanist debate to resolve these conflicts.

An anxious future is ahead as we approach the ability to screen for genetic deafness, and then possibly to alter a child's genetic makeup. When the day arrives that women can find out from an amniocentesis whether their children are Deaf, what will the moral and cultural environment be? How will Deaf people act when faced with knowledge about what traits their unborn children have? Our consolation may be that when that day comes, Deaf people will not be alone. Many others will be just as conflicted, including women who will be faced with a decision about their unborn children with other "undesirable" traits. The day a "deafness gene" can be altered is the same day that other genetic conditions can also be altered, so in this area of technology at least, Deaf people will find allies—as they do today with disabled people and ethnic groups—in their search for a humanist approach to scientific knowledge.

What do Deaf people want from the future? What they have always wanted and what every culture and linguistic community wants: a preservation of their sign language and their ways of being. This does not mean that they expect things to remain the same. It does mean that they want to be free of inhumane threats from technological and biological "solutions" to their existence. They still may well embrace technology as they do with devices that expand their ability to exploit human voice to their advantage. Cochlear implants may become useful to Deaf people in the way that hearing aids have been to many. Deaf people may be delighted to be able to predict with certainty that their offspring will or will not be deaf. They may end up making substantial moral and ethical contributions to the Human Genome Project, and help guide humanist approaches to genetic knowledge. The problem for

Deaf people is, as always, how to articulate their views of science and knowledge in a world that finds it easier *not* to understand them.

There is a final lesson from the history of Deaf people: Without diversity of culture, language, and different ways of seeing the world, we would never have learned what we now know about the different ways that humans live. The linguistic and social lives of Deaf people have provided us with unique and valuable ways of exploring the vast potential for human language and culture.

Notes

Acknowledgments

Index

Notes

Introduction

1. J. Woodward, *How You Gonna Get to Heaven if You Can't Talk with Jesus: On Depathologizing Deafness* (Silver Spring, MD: TJ Publishers, 1982). For example, we use the lowercase "deaf" when referring to schools for the deaf or classrooms for deaf children in public schools because the standard for placement of children is by hearing loss. We use the uppercase "Deaf" when referring to institutions built by Deaf people such as Deaf clubs, Deaf churches, and Deaf organizations as well as when describing those individuals who share in this social history.
2. G. Veditz, *Proceedings of the Ninth Convention of the National Association of the Deaf and the Third World Congress of the Deaf, 1910* (Philadelphia: Philocophus Press, 1912), 30.
3. A. Kuper, *Culture: The Anthropologists' Account* (Cambridge, MA: Harvard University Press, 1999), 14.
4. C. Geertz, *The Interpretation of Cultures: Selected Essays* (New York: Basic Books, 1974), 45.
5. A. Martinez, J. Linden, L. Schimmenti, and C. Pauler, "Attitudes of the Broader Hearing, Deaf and Hard-of-Hearing Community toward Genetic Testing for Deafness," *Genetics in Medicine* 5 (2003).
6. J. Clifford, *The Predicament of Culture: Twentieth-Century Ethnography, Literature, and Art* (Cambridge, MA: Harvard University Press, 1988), 9.

1. Silenced Bodies

1. K. Kritz, "The Maryland School for the Deaf," *Maryland Bulletin* (Mar. 1991).

2. A. Schildroth, "Recent Changes in the Educational Placement of Deaf Students," *American Annals of the Deaf* 133 (1988).

3. Gallaudet Research Institute, *Regional and National Summary Report of Data from the 2001–2002 Annual Survey of Deaf and Hard-of-Hearing Children and Youth* (Washington: GRI, Gallaudet University, 2003).

4. C. Ramsey and C. Padden, "Natives and Newcomers: Literacy Education for Deaf Children," *Anthropology and Education Quarterly* 29 (1998).

5. E. A. Fay, "Tabular Statement of American Schools for the Deaf, 1889," *American Annals of the Deaf and Dumb* 35 (1890).

6. H. Lane, *When the Mind Hears: A History of the Deaf* (New York: Random House, 1984); J. Van Cleve and B. Crouch, *A Place of Their Own: Creating the Deaf Community in America* (Washington: Gallaudet University Press, 1989).

7. D. C. Baynton, *Forbidden Signs: American Culture and the Campaign against Sign Language* (Chicago: University of Chicago Press, 1996); Lane, *When the Mind Hears;* Van Cleve and Crouch, *A Place of Their Own.*

8. H. Van Allen, *A Brief History of the Pennsylvania Institution for the Deaf and Dumb* (Mt. Airy, PA: Board of Directors of the Pennsylvania Institution for the Deaf and Dumb, 1893).

9. J. Gannon, *Deaf Heritage: A Narrative History of Deaf America* (Silver Spring, MD: National Association of the Deaf, 1981).

10. D. J. Rothman, *The Discovery of the Asylum: Social Order and Disorder in the New Republic,* rev. ed. (Boston: Little, Brown, 1990).

11. R. N. Ryon, "Roberts Vaux: A Biography of a Reformer," Ph.D. diss., Pennsylvania State University, 1966, 36.

12. M. Ignatieff, "State, Civil Society and Total Institutions: A Critique of Recent Social Histories of Punishment," in *Social Control and the State: Historical and Comparative Essays,* ed. S. Cohen and A. T. Scull (Oxford: Robertson, 1983).

13. Rothman, *Discovery of the Asylum.*

14. Lane, *When the Mind Hears.*

15. Ignatieff, "State, Civil Society and Total Institutions," 81.

16. Van Allen, *A Brief History,* 4.

17. Pennsylvania Institution for the Deaf and Dumb, *An Account of the Origin and Progress of the Pennsylvania Institution for the Deaf and Dumb* (Philadelphia: W. Fry, 1821).

18. Ryon, "Roberts Vaux."

19. R. R. Bell, *The Philadelphia Lawyer: A History, 1735–1945* (London: Associated University Presses, 1992); W. D. Lewis, *Great American Lawyers, the*

Lives and Influence of Judges and Lawyers Who Have Acquired Permanent National Reputation, and Have Developed the Jurisprudence of the United States: A History of the Legal Profession in America (South Hackensack, NJ: Rothman Reprints, 1971).

20. E. Wolf, *History of the Jews of Philadelphia from Colonial Times to the Age of Jackson* (Philadelphia: Jewish Publishing, 1975).

21. Pennsylvania Institution for the Deaf and Dumb, *An Account of the Origin and Progress of the Pennsylvania Institution for the Deaf and Dumb.*

22. Ryon, "Roberts Vaux."

23. Board of Directors of the Pennsylvania Institution for the Deaf and Dumb, Committee of Instruction Report, Mar. 7, 1821, Pennsylvania School for the Deaf Archives, Gallaudet University Library, Washington, D.C. (hereafter Pennsylvania School for the Deaf Archives).

24. Pennsylvania Institution for the Deaf and Dumb, *An Account of the Origin and Progress of the Pennsylvania Institution for the Deaf and Dumb*, 24.

25. Ibid.

26. Board of Directors of the Pennsylvania Institution for the Deaf and Dumb, Committee of Instruction Report.

27. Meeting of the Female Committee of the Pennsylvania Institution for the Deaf and Dumb, Jan. 8, 1821, Pennsylvania School for the Deaf Archives.

28. Van Allen, *A Brief History.*

29. Board of Directors of the Pennsylvania Institution for the Deaf and Dumb, Minutes of the Pennsylvania Institution for the Deaf and Dumb, Nov. 7, 1821, Pennsylvania School for the Deaf Archives.

30. Board of Directors of the Pennsylvania Institution for the Deaf and Dumb, Minutes of the Pennsylvania Institution for the Deaf and Dumb, Sept. 27, 1821, Pennsylvania School for the Deaf Archives.

31. Board of Directors of the Pennsylvania Institution for the Deaf and Dumb, Minutes of the Pennsylvania Institution for the Deaf and Dumb, Nov. 7, 1821.

32. Ibid.

33. Ibid.

34. David Seixas to the President and Directors of the Pennsylvania Institution for the Deaf and Dumb, Oct. 29, 1821, Pennsylvania School for the Deaf Archives.

35. Board of Directors of the Pennsylvania Institution for the Deaf and Dumb, Minutes of the Pennsylvania Institution for the Deaf and Dumb, Oct. 3, 1821, Pennsylvania School for the Deaf Archives.

36. Board of Directors of the Pennsylvania Institution for the Deaf and Dumb, Minutes of the Pennsylvania Institution for the Deaf and Dumb, Nov. 3, 1821, Pennsylvania School for the Deaf Archives.

37. Wolf, *History of the Jews of Philadelphia*, 336.

38. Ibid., 336.

39. Ryon, "Roberts Vaux."

40. Rothman, *Discovery of the Asylum*, 83.

41. Ryon, "Roberts Vaux," 125.

42. Committee of Instruction, Report to the Directors of the Pennsylvania Institute for the Deaf and Dumb, Mar. 7, 1821, Pennsylvania Institution for the Deaf and Dumb, Philadelphia.

43. Ibid.

44. Ignatieff, "State, Civil Society and Total Institution."

45. M. Foucault and P. Rabinow, *The Foucault Reader* (New York: Pantheon, 1984), 324.

46. Pennsylvania Institution for the Deaf and Dumb, *An Account of the Origin and Progress of the Pennsylvania Institute for the Deaf and Dumb*.

47. Foucault and Rabinow, *Foucault Reader*, 154.

48. G. Kesich, "State Ready to Pay Victims of Abuse," *Portland Press Herald*, Nov. 26, 2001.

49. Foucault and Rabinow, *Foucault Reader*, 152.

50. E. Laborit, *The Cry of the Gull* (Washington: Gallaudet University Press, 1998), 117.

51. Van Allen, *A Brief History*.

2. An Entirely Separate School

1. J. Brasington, *The South Carolina School for the Deaf and the Blind: 1849–1999* (Spartanburg: South Carolina School for the Deaf and the Blind, 2000).

2. G. Robinson, Class of 1952, videotape documentary, Gallaudet University, Department of Television, Film and Photography, Washington, DC.

3. Guide to the Resting Places of the Founders of the American School for the Deaf, Hartford, CT, American School for the Deaf.

4. Annual Report to the State Legislature, 1864, South Carolina Institution for the Deaf and the Blind, Spartanburg.

5. Annual Report to the State Legislature, 1888, South Carolina Institution for the Deaf and the Blind, Spartanburg.

6. E. Hairston and L. Smith, *Black and Deaf in America: Are We That Different?* (Silver Spring, MD: TJ Publishers, 1983).

7. D. C. Baynton, *Forbidden Signs: American Culture and the Campaign against Sign Language* (Chicago: University of Chicago Press, 1996), fn. 35.

8. A. Bickley, *In Spite of Obstacles: A History of the West Virginia Schools for the Colored Deaf and Blind, 1926–1955* (Charleston: West Virginia Department of Education and the Arts, Division of Rehabilitation Service, 2001); M. Crockett and B. Dease, *Through the Years, 1867–1977: Light Out of Darkness* (Raleigh, NC: Barefoot Press, 1990).

9. R. Bass, *History of the State School for the Deaf and the Blind, Hampton, Virginia* (Hampton, VA: State School for the Deaf and the Blind, 1978).

10. W. B. Edgar, *South Carolina: A History* (Columbia: University of South Carolina Press, 1998); J. Underwood and W. L. Burke, eds., *At Freedom's Door: African-American Founding Fathers and Lawyers in Reconstruction South Carolina* (Columbia: University of South Carolina Press, 2000).

11. J. K. Jillson to N. F. Walker, Sept. 1, 1873, in Education Records: J. K. Jillson Correspondence General, vol. 13, South Carolina Department of Archives and History, Columbia.

12. Ibid.

13. J. K. Jillson to N. F. Walker, Sept. 27 and Sept. 29, 1873, in Education Records: J. K. Jillson Correspondence General, vol. 13.

14. Edgar, *South Carolina*, 386.

15. Underwood and Burke, *At Freedom's Door*.

16. Minutes of the Board of Commissioners of the South Carolina Institute for the Deaf, Dumb and Blind, Feb. 13, 1879, Cedar Spring.

17. Minutes of the Board of Commissioners of the South Carolina Institute for the Deaf, Dumb and Blind, June 13, 1883, Cedar Spring.

18. Minutes of the Board of Commissioners of the South Carolina Institute for the Deaf, Dumb and Blind, Aug. 8, 1882, Cedar Spring.

19. Board of Commissioners, Annual Report of the South Carolina Institution for the Deaf, Dumb and Blind, Aug. 8, 1882, Cedar Spring.

20. Brasington, *South Carolina School for the Deaf and the Blind*.

21. G. Bowker and L. Star, *Sorting Things Out: Classification and Its Consequences* (Cambridge, MA: MIT Press, 1999), 10.

22. Board of Commissioners, Annual Report of the South Carolina Institution for the Deaf, Dumb and Blind, Aug. 8, 1882.

23. Ibid.

24. Minutes of the Board of Commissioners of the South Carolina Institute for the Deaf, Dumb and Blind, Aug. 14, 1889, Cedar Spring.

25. T. Carter, "Notes," *The Palmetto Leaf*, May 8, 1897.

26. Baynton, *Forbidden Signs*; J. Van Cleve and B. Crouch, *A Place of Their*

Own: Creating the Deaf Community in America (Washington: Gallaudet University Press, 1989).

27. Van Allen, *Brief History*.
28. D. C. Baynton, "Savages and Deaf-Mutes: Evolutionary Theory and the Campaign against Sign Language," in *Anthropology and Human Movement II: Searching for Origins,* ed. Drid Williams (Lanham, MD: Scarecrow Press, 1999).
29. Baynton, *Forbidden Signs*.
30. Minutes of the Board of Commissioners of the South Carolina Institute for the Deaf, Dumb and Blind, Aug. 14, 1889.
31. Van Cleve and Crouch, *A Place of Their Own*.
32. Van Allen, *Brief History,* 24.
33. H. Joyner, *From Pity to Pride: Growing up Deaf in the Old South* (Washington: Gallaudet University Press, 2004).
34. Crockett and Dease, *Through the Years*.
35. Interview with Ernest Hairston, Aug. 23, 2002.
36. M. H. Wright, *Sounds Like Home: Growing Up Black and Deaf in the South* (Washington: Gallaudet University Press, 1999).
37. Baynton, *Forbidden Signs*.
38. Bickley, *In Spite of Obstacles*.
39. Crockett and Dease, *Through the Years,* 210–211.
40. *Miller et al. v. Board of Education of District of Columbia et al.,* United States District Court for the District of Columbia, 1952.
41. Robinson, Class of 1952, videotape documentary.
42. Ibid.

3. The Problem of Voice

1. *Deaf Mute Girl Reciting "The Star Spangled Banner"* (American Mutoscope and Biograph Company, 1902), film.
2. C. Harpole, *History of the American Cinema* (New York: Scribner's, 1990).
3. O. Regensburg, "Report of the Motion Picture Fund Committee," *Proceedings of the Tenth Convention of the National Association of the Deaf,* Cleveland, Ohio, Aug. 20, 1913, 98.
4. Ibid.; G. Veditz, *The Preservation of the Sign Language* (Silver Spring, MD: National Association of the Deaf, 1913), film.
5. J. Van Cleve, "Nebraska's Oral Law of 1911 and the Deaf Community," *Nebraska History* 65 (1984); J. Van Cleve and B. Crouch, *A Place of Their Own: Creating the Deaf Community in America* (Washington: Gallaudet University Press, 1989).

6. Van Cleve and Crouch, *A Place of Their Own*.

7. N. Frishberg, "Arbitrariness and Iconicity: Historical Change in American Sign Language," *Language* 51 (1975).

8. *The Preservation of American Sign Language: The Complete Historical Collection* (Burtonsville, MD: Sign Media, 1997), videotape.

9. George Veditz to Roy Stewart, Mar. 29, 1915, Roy Stewart Papers, Gallaudet University Library, Washington, DC. (hereafter Roy Stewart Papers).

10. Edward Miner Gallaudet to Roy Stewart, May 29, 1911, Roy Stewart Papers.

11. George Veditz to Roy Stewart, Mar. 29, 1915.

12. Ibid.

13. I. Bjorlee, "Tributes: George William Veditz," *Maryland Bulletin* 57 (1937); M. Garretson, "The Veditz Genius," *Silent Worker* 3 (1951); G. Veditz, "An Old Timer's Autobiography," *Maryland Bulletin* 44 (1924).

14. Bjorlee, "Tributes"; J. Fernandes and J. Fernandes, *Signs of Eloquence: Foundations of Deaf American Public Address* (San Diego, CA: Dawn Sign Press, forthcoming).

15. M. Olson and J. Van Cleve, "Preservation Serendipity: The Gallaudet University Archives and the Veditz Transcription," *Sign Language Studies* 4 (2004).

16. J. Gannon, "A Tribute to Roy J. Stewart: He Helped Make Our Sign Language Immortal," *Sign Language Studies* 4 (2004).

17. Anton Schroeder to Roy Stewart, Jan. 10, 1914, Roy Stewart Papers.

18. J. Schulyer Long to Roy Stewart, Mar. 26, 1915, Roy Stewart Papers.

19. T. Supalla, "The Validity of the Gallaudet Lecture Films," *Sign Language Studies* 4 (2004).

20. George Veditz to Roy Stewart, Mar. 29, 1915.

21. Anton Schroeder to Roy Stewart, Jan. 10, 1914.

22. J. Gannon, *Deaf Heritage: A Narrative History of Deaf America* (Silver Spring, MD: National Association of the Deaf, 1981); Van Cleve, "Nebraska's Oral Law of 1911 and the Deaf Community."

23. J. Schulyer Long to Roy Stewart, Mar. 26, 1915.

24. D. C. Baynton, "Savages and Deaf-Mutes: Evolutionary Theory and the Campaign against Sign Language" in *Anthropology and Human Movement II: Searching for Origins*, ed. Drid Williams (Lanham, MD: Scarecrow Press, 1999).

25. D. C. Baynton, *Forbidden Signs: American Culture and the Campaign against Sign Language* (Chicago: University of Chicago Press, 1996).

26. D. Freedman, "Enrollment in Sign Language Classes Swells," *Associated*

Press, May 13, 2002; Report on Foreign Language Enrollments in United States Institutions of Higher Education, Fall 2002, Modern Language Association, New York.

27. M. Daniels, *Dancing with Words: Signing for Hearing Children's Literacy* (Westport, CT: Bergin & Garvey, 2001).

28. Annual Survey of Hearing Impaired Children and Youth, report, Gallaudet University, Washington, DC.

29. J. Christiansen and I. Leigh, *Cochlear Implants in Children: Ethics and Choices* (Washington: Gallaudet University Press, 2002).

30. G. Toppo, "Teens Grasp Sign Language; ASL Classes Seen as Less 'Foreign' Alternative," *USA Today,* Dec. 10, 2002.

4. A New Class Consciousness

1. D. Miles, "A History of Theatre Activities in the Deaf Community of the United States," master's thesis, Connecticut College, 1974.

2. J. DeBee, *The LACD Story* (Los Angeles: Beyond Sound, 1985), film; T. Supalla, *Charles Krauel: Profile of a Deaf Filmmaker* (San Diego: Dawn Sign Press, 1992), film.

3. Interview with John Bradley, Emil Hartley, and Louis Ferraro, Apr. 20, 2002.

4. Interviews with Oscar Cohen, Feb. 6, 2002, and Gerald Burstein, Feb. 9, 2000; J. Mitchell, "The Deaf-Mutes' Club," *Up in the Old Hotel* (New York: Vintage, 1993).

5. B. Burnes, "The Race Question," *Silent Worker,* Jan. 1950, 15.

6. E. Hairston and L. Smith, *Black and Deaf in America: Are We That Different?* (Silver Spring, MD: TJ Publishers, 1983); interview with Charles Williams, July 10, 2002.

7. R. M. Buchanan, *Illusions of Equality: Deaf Americans in School and Factory, 1850–1950* (Washington: Gallaudet University Press, 1999); L. Schreiber, "Those Firestone Folks," *Silent Worker,* Jan. 1950.

8. Interview with Charles Williams, July 10, 2002.

9. B. Bragg and E. Bergman, *Tales from a Clubroom* (Washington: Gallaudet University Press, 1981).

10. A. L. Roberts, "The Editor's Page," *Frat* 45 (1948): 4.

11. B. Graham, *One Thing Led to the Next: The Real History of TTYs* (Evanston, IL: Mosquito Publishing, 1988).

12. Summary of State Telecommunications Relay Services, Gallaudet University, Washington, DC, 1992.

13. Buchanan, *Illusions of Equality.*

14. H. Allen, *Rubber's Home Town* (New York: Stratford House, 1949).

15. Interview with John Bradley, Emil Hartley, and Louis Ferraro, Apr. 20, 2002.

16. Allen, *Rubber's Home Town.*

17. Buchanan, *Illusions of Equality.*

18. Interview with Roger Scott, May 21, 2002.

19. S. Lipset, M. Trow, and J. Coleman, *Union Democracy: The Internal Politics of the International Typographical Union* (Glencoe, IL: Free Press, 1956).

20. Ibid.

21. J. Gannon, *Deaf Heritage: A Narrative History of Deaf America* (Silver Spring, MD: National Association of the Deaf, 1981).

22. Interview with Merv Garretson, May 21, 2002.

23. W. Leach, *Country of Exiles: The Destruction of Place in American Life* (New York: Pantheon, 1999).

24. B. Burnes, "The Editor's Page," *Silent Worker,* 1950, 2.

5. Technology of Voice

1. E. A. Fay, "Miscellaneous: How *Dumb* Was Dropped," *American Annals of the Deaf and Dumb* 34 (1889): 82.

2. Ibid., 157–158.

3. J. DeBee, *The LACD Story* (Los Angeles, 1985), film.

4. T. Supalla, *Charles Krauel: Profile of a Deaf Filmmaker* (San Diego: Dawn Sign Press, 1992), film.

5. D. Miles, "A History of Theatre Activities in the Deaf Community of the United States," master's thesis, Connecticut College, 1974.

6. Ibid.

7. Interview with Bernard Bragg, Nov. 15, 2001.

8. D. Lifson, *The Yiddish Theatre in America* (New York: Thomas Yoseloff, 1965).

9. Interview with Eric Malzkuhn, Dec. 26, 2001.

10. S. Baldwin, *Pictures in the Air* (Washington: Gallaudet University Press, 1993); ibid.

11. Baldwin, *Pictures in the Air.*

12. Bernard Bragg to David Hays, Oct. 28, 1966, personal collection of Bernard Bragg.

13. David Hays to Bernard Bragg, June 10, 1966, personal collection of Bernard Bragg.

14. D. Hays, "An Experiment in Television," Feb. 1967, NBC, New York.

15. Baldwin, *Pictures in the Air.*

16. C. Barnes, "Stage: The Special Talents of Theater of the Deaf," *New York Times,* Feb. 25, 1969.
17. Interview with Patrick Graybill, July 10, 2002.
18. H. S. Becker, *Art Worlds* (Berkeley: University of California Press, 1982).
19. Baldwin, *Pictures in the Air,* 23.
20. S. DuBow, *Legal Rights: The Guide for Deaf and Hard of Hearing People,* 5th ed. (Washington: Gallaudet University Press, 2000).
21. Summary of State Telecommunications Relay Services (Washington: National Center for Law and Deafness, Gallaudet University, 1992).
22. J. Grigeley, White Noise (New York, 2000), graphite on paper, pins.

6. Anxiety of Culture

1. W. Stokoe, C. Croneberg, and D. Casterline, *A Dictionary of American Sign Language on Linguistic Principles* (Washington: Gallaudet University Press, 1965).
2. W. Stokoe, "Sign Language Structure: An Outline of the Visual Communication Systems of the American Deaf," *Studies in Linguistics, Occasional Papers* 8 (1960).
3. F. J. Newmeyer, *The Politics of Linguistics* (Chicago: University of Chicago Press, 1986).
4. See K. Emmorey, *Language, Cognition and the Brain: Insights from Sign Language Research* (Mahwah, NJ: Lawrence Erlbaum, 2002); K. Emmorey and H. Lane, *The Signs of Language Revisited: An Anthology to Honor Ursula Bellugi and Edward Klima* (Mahwah, NJ: Lawrence Erlbaum, 2000); R. Meier, K. Cormier, and D. Quinto-Pozos, *Modality and Structure in Signed and Spoken Languages* (Cambridge: Cambridge University Press, 2002).
5. L. Fant, *Ameslan: An Introduction to American Sign Language* (Northridge, CA: Joyce Motion Picture Co., 1972).
6. C. Padden and D. Clark, "How the Alphabet Came to Be Used in a Sign Language," *Sign Language Studies* 4 (2003).
7. J. C. Woodward, "Some Characteristics of Pidgin Sign English," *Sign Language Studies* 3 (1973).
8. W. C. Stokoe, "Sign Language Diglossia," *Studies in Linguistics* 21 (1970).
9. D. Anthony, *The Seeing Essential English Code-Breaker* (Greeley: University of Colorado Bookstore, 1974); G. Gustason, G. Pfetzing, and E. Zawolkow, *Signing Exact English* (Silver Spring, MD: Modern Signs Press, 1975).
10. G. Gustason, ed., *Signing English: Exact or Not?* (Los Alamitos, CA: Modern Signs Press, 1988).

11. L. Lawson, "Do We Want One or Multiple Deaf Nations?," *Deaf Worlds* 18, no. 3 (2002).

12. S. Baldwin, *Pictures in the Air* (Washington: Gallaudet University Press, 1993).

13. D. Miles, *Poetry Demonstration* (La Jolla, CA: Salk Institute, 1975), videotape.

14. D. Miles, *Gestures: Poetry in Sign Language* (Los Angeles: Joyce Motion Picture Co., 1976).

15. M. Garretson, *Words from a Deaf Child and Other Verses* (Silver Spring, MD: Fragonard Press, 1984), R. Panara, T. Denis, and J. McFarlane, eds., *The Silent Muse: An Anthology of Prose and Poetry by the Deaf* (Washington: Gallaudet College Alumni Association, 1960).

16. D. Miles, *Poetry Demonstration II* (La Jolla, CA: Salk Institute, 1976), videotape.

17. Ibid.

18. M. Davidson, "Hearing Things: The Scandal of Speech in Deaf Performance," in *Signing the Body Poetic: Essays on American Sign Language Literature*, ed. D. Bauman, J. Nelson, and H. Rose (Berkeley: University of California Press, forthcoming).

19. E. Lentz, *The Treasure: Poems by Ella Mae Lentz* (Oakland, CA: In Motion Press, 1995), video.

20. Davidson, "Hearing Things."

21. C. Krentz, "The Camera as Printing Press: How Film Has Impacted ASL Literature," in *Signing the Body Poetic*, ed. Bauman, Nelson, and Rose.

22. P. Cook and K. Lerner, *Flying Words Project* (La Jolla, CA: UCSD-Television, 2001), video.

7. The Promise of Culture

1. C. Padden and H. Markowicz, "Learning to Be Deaf: Conflicts between Hearing and Deaf Cultures," in *Mind, Culture, and Activity*, ed. M. Cole, Y. Engeström, and O. Vasquez (New York: Cambridge University Press, 1997), 418–431; J. C. Woodward, "Some Characteristics of Pidgin Sign English," *Sign Language Studies* 3 (1973): 39–46.

2. W. Stokoe, C. Croneberg, and D. Casterline, *A Dictionary of American Sign Language on Linguistic Principles* (Washington: Gallaudet University Press, 1965).

3. J. Clifford, *The Predicament of Culture: Twentieth-Century Ethnography, Literature, and Art* (Cambridge, MA: Harvard University Press, 1988).

8. Cultures into the Future

1. Report on Foreign Language Enrollments in United States Institutions of Higher Education, Fall 2002, Nov. 6, 2003, Modern Language Association, New York.
2. E. A. Fay, "Tabular Statement of American Schools for the Deaf, 1889," *American Annals of the Deaf and Dumb* 35 (1890): 57–65.
3. J. Christiansen and I. Leigh, *Cochlear Implants in Children: Ethics and Choices* (Washington: Gallaudet University Press, 2002).
4. GLAD Position Paper on Cochlear Implants, Greater Los Angeles Association of the Deaf, Los Angeles, CA, 1985.
5. Christiansen and Leigh, *Cochlear Implants in Children*, 264; H. Lane, "Cochlear Implants: Boon for Some—Bane for Others," *Hearing Health* Feb./Mar. (1993).
6. Christiansen and Leigh, *Cochlear Implants in Children*, 262–263.
7. R. Weisberg, *Sound and Fury* (New York: Filmmakers' Library, 2000).
8. A. P. Aiello and M. Aiello, "Cochlear Implants and Deaf Identity," in *Deaf World: A Historical Reader and Primary Sourcebook*, ed. L. Bragg (New York: New York University Press, 1999).
9. R. I. Mayberry, "The Importance of Childhood to Language Acquisition: Evidence from American Sign Language," in *The Development of Speech Perception: The Transition from Speech Sounds to Spoken Words*, ed. Judith C. Goodman et al. (Cambridge, MA: MIT Press, 1994). R. I. Mayberry and E. B. Eichen, "The Long-Lasting Advantage of Learning Sign Language in Childhood: Another Look at the Critical Period for Language Acquisition," *Journal of Memory and Language* 30 (1991).
10. K. Arnos and A. Pandya, "Advances in the Genetics of Deafness," in *Oxford Handbook of Deaf Studies, Language, and Education*, ed. M. Marschark and P. E. Spencer (New York: Oxford University Press, 2003).
11. Unknown, "He Got the Star: Being the Story of a Youth Who Hitched His Wagon to a Star," *Silent Worker* 5 (1953).
12. B. Teitelbaum, "Stan," *Silent Worker* 5 (1953).
13. Unknown, "Louisiana Beautician Makes Good," *Silent Worker* 5 (1953).
14. B. Teitelbaum, "Edwin Meade Hazel: The Silent Worker Parliamentarian Is Also a Mechanical Wizard," *Silent Worker* 5 (1953).
15. L. M. Jacobs and A. Watson, "Personalities in Phoenix, Arizona," *Silent Worker* 5 (1953).
16. J. Van Cleve and B. Crouch, *A Place of Their Own: Creating the Deaf Community in America* (Washington: Gallaudet University Press, 1989).

17. B. Greenwald, "The Real 'Toll' of A. G. Bell: Lessons about Eugenics," in *Genetics, Disability and Deafness*, ed. J. VanCleve (Washington: Gallaudet University Press, forthcoming).
18. S. Snyder and D. Miller, eds., *Cultural Locations of Disability* (Ann Arbor: University of Michigan Press, forthcoming 2005).
19. A. Johansson, *Resurrecting Sound* (Washington: Gallaudet University, Department of Film, Video and Photography, 2002), video; Christiansen and Leigh, *Cochlear Implants in Children*.

Acknowledgments

When we began working on this book, we knew we would have to draw on the personal histories of Deaf people as well as on archival materials. We were fortunate to have friends and colleagues who could illuminate the past for us; they agreed to sit with us for interviews and to tolerate our quizzing them about their lives in deaf schools, their experiences in the workplace, and what they remembered about Gallaudet, Deaf clubs, and Deaf theaters. To those whose time and patience we taxed the most, we give our deepest thanks: Glenn Anderson, Yerker and Nancy Andersson, Cindy O'Grady Batch, Gerald "Bummy" Bernstein, Bernard Bragg, Gil Eastman, Jack and Rosalyn Gannon, Merv and Carol Garretson, Patrick Graybill, Ernie Hairston, Marla Hatrak, Jerald and Shirley Jordan, Eric Malzkuhn, Nathie Marbury, Jane Norman, Roger Scott, Babs Stevens, Frank Turk, Kay Vincent, and Barbara Willigan.

To fill in the gaps, we often called on Carol's parents, Agnes and Don Padden, to remember and search personal records for details of who, when, and where. When they didn't know, they directed us to one of their many friends and acquaintances. They stood ready to drive from their home in Frederick, Maryland, to Gallaudet University Library Archives to pick up materials urgently needed for research. Carol's brother and sister-in-law, Bob and Melinda Padden, helped with research on George Veditz, drawing from the archives at the Maryland School for the Deaf.

Michael Olson's thorough and exhaustive knowledge of every corner of the Gallaudet University Library Archives was a precious resource to us. Mike's fortuitous discovery of the Roy Stewart correspondence, which included many long-lost letters between Roy Stewart and George Veditz, directly influenced the third chapter of this book. We appreciate the assistance of Marion Chandler and Garry Davis, two entirely capable archivists of the South Carolina Department of Archives and History. Without their help, we would not have been able to fill in the details of post–Civil War South Carolina and the state's education of Black and white deaf children. We are also grateful to Superintendent Sheila Breitweiser of the South Carolina School for the Deaf and the Blind and Headmaster Joseph Fischgrund of the Pennsylvania School for the Deaf for allowing us access to their archives. Their generous assistance demonstrates above all that a history or rather, histories, of Deaf people concern us all.

For material we could not find in any archive, particularly about Deaf men and women working during and after the Second World War, details of silent Deaf theaters, and Black deaf schools, we thank Evon Black, John Bradley, Jr., Oscar Cohen, Harvey Corson, Lindsay Dunn, Louis Ferrara, Ben Finkle, Emil Hartman, Barbara Kannapell, Paddy Ladd, Francine and Iosep MacDougall, Carolyn McCaskill, Tom McKenna, Martha Saunders, Leah Subak, Ted Supalla, Marva Turner, and Chuck and Pat Williams.

The John Simon Guggenheim Foundation provided a fellowship to Carol that enabled her to begin doing research for the book. Glenn Anderson, Douglas Baynton, Jack Gannon, Harlan Lane, Richard Meier, and John Van Cleve, along with an anonymous reader, provided enormously helpful suggestions and corrections to an early version. Our writing is much improved because of the quality of their assistance to us. Carol's graduate students Susan Sterne and Jennifer Rayman helped with early stages of research for this book. Mala Kleinfeld and Bonnie Sherwood assisted with necessary details of our manuscript. Elizabeth Knoll, our editor, supplied both patience and a sense of urgency, and Julie Carlson skillfully and sensitively edited our words.

Index

African-Americans: segregation and, 37–38, 40–47, 50–52, 54–56; employment and, 40–41, 81; enfranchisement of, 42–43; voting power of, 42–43; Jillson and, 42–44; manual labor and, 47; *Brown v. Board of Education* and, 52–53; Gallaudet University and, 53–54; NAD and, 80; sports and, 81; deaf clubs and, 85–86

Akron Club for the Deaf, 88

Alphabet cards, 84

American Annals of the Deaf and Dumb, 41, 73, 100

American Association to Promote the Teaching of Speech to the Deaf, 59

American Breeders Association, 176

American Postal Workers' Union, 117

American School for the Deaf, 39, 42, 60, 63

American Sign Language (ASL), 2–4, 56, 75; Canada and, 3, 9; United States and, 9; New York P.S. 47 and, 36; films and, 57–64; fingerspelling and, 61–62; changes in, 67–69; grammar and, 98; increase of, 115; naming issues over, 126–130, 154–155; vocabulary invention and, 128–129; poets and, 131–132; storytellers and, 131–132; identity and, 150–151, 160–162; public interest in, 157–160; popularity of, 163

Americans with Disabilities Act, 116–117

Ameslan, 126

Amniocentesis, 179

Anderson, Glenn, 81

Anderson, Jessie, Jr., 44

Arsenic and Old Lace (play), 104–105

Association of the Friends for the Instruction of the Poor, 20

Asylums, 12, 18; power and, 30–31; Foucault and, 30–32; centralized, 48–49. *See also* Deaf schools

Bache, Franklin, 20

Bahan, Ben, 132, 137

Bancroft, Anne, 109

Barnes, Clive, 112–113

Baynton, Douglas, 48, 73–74

Becker, Howard, 113

Bell, Alexander Graham, 48, 59, 174–176; *Memoir upon the Formation of a Deaf Variety of the Human Race*, 174–175